PORTRAITS OF JESUS

Matthew

PORTRAITS OF JESUS

Matthew

A CONTEXTUAL APPROACH
to Bible Study

by
William Domeris

COLLINS

Collins Liturgical Publications
8 Grafton Street, London W1X 3LA

Collins Liturgical in USA
Icehouse One — 401
151 Union Street, San Francisco, CA 94111-1299

Collins Liturgical in Canada
Novalis, Box 9700, Terminal
375 Rideau St, Ottawa, Ontario K1G 4B4

Distributed in Ireland by
Educational Company of Ireland
21 Talbot Street, Dublin 1

Collins Liturgical Australia
PO Box 316, Blackburn, Victoria 3130

Collins Liturgical New Zealand
PO Box 1, Auckland

ISBN 0 00 599974 X
© 1987 text William Domeris, illustrations Wm Collins

First published 1987

Cover illustration by Velile Soha
Cover design by Malcolm Harvey Young
Typographical design by Colin Reed
Typeset by John Swain & Son Limited
Made and printed in Great Britain
by Collins, Glasgow

Library of Congress Cataloging-in-Publication Data

Domeris, William.
    Portraits of Jesus: Matthew.

    1. Jesus Christ — History of doctrines — Early church, ca. 30-600.
    2. Bible. N.T. Matthew — Criticism, interpretation, etc.
    3. Bible. N.T. Matthew — Study.   I. Bible. N.T. Matthew.   II. Title.
BT198-D63 1988   226'.206   87-18295
ISBN 0-00-599974-X (pbk.)

Contents

General Introduction

This study is part of a series of commentaries on the four gospels. The aim of the series is to present the distinct portrait of Jesus which each gospel provides, and yet to do so in a way which shows how the four portraits relate to and complement each other. None of the volumes is therefore intended to be a comprehensive commentary on a particular gospel. The passages chosen for study and reflection have been selected because they portray most vividly the portrait which the evangelist wishes to paint. Yet, when all four volumes are taken as a whole, it will be seen that they cover a great deal of the material found in the four gospels.

The origin of the series is important for understanding what has been attempted. Each of the four authors is a biblical scholar well versed in the contemporary discussion on the gospels. In particular, each has a special interest in the sociology of the New Testament and a contextual approach to Christian faith and theology. Even though much scholarly work lies behind each volume, the authors have not sought to engage in scholarly debate. They have provided, rather, commentaries for use in Bible study groups and by people at the 'grass-roots'. Indeed, the commentaries originated as much within such groups as they did within the scholar's study. For several months each author met with various Bible study groups comprised of people from different denominational, racial and socio-economic backgrounds. Together they explored the gospels in order to discern who Jesus really is for us today. Hence the attempt to locate the portrait of Jesus in three contexts or horizons: his own context; the context of the original evangelist and those to whom the gospel was written; and our own situation today. Each of these is pertinent to understanding who Jesus is for us, and they also provide a way into the study of the gospels which has already proved useful in Bible study groups.

The authors have worked as a team, and each of the four volumes follow a similar pattern. All have used the New International Version of the Bible, and, as already indicated, a premium has been placed by all on a sociological approach to the text. Each volume also contains suggestions as to how they can best be used. There is, therefore, a basic structure common to all four volumes. Yet each author has brought to the task different insights and experiences, gained, not least, from discussing the gospels with people who are struggling in different contexts to be faithful to Jesus Christ in South Africa. This, rather than some rigid formula, has shaped the final product. It is our hope that other Bible study groups will find them of value and use for their own journey of faith and obedience within their particular historical and social context. Our overriding concern is that each person discover the Jesus to whom the four evangelists bear witness.

John W. de Gruchy
Bill Domeris
General Editors

Introduction: Framing the Portrait

Three horizons

Welcome to the world of Matthew's Gospel! As we read the Gospel together, we will become aware of the blending of three different settings or horizons.

The *first* of these is the world of Jesus. The Gospel is full of information about Jesus, what he said, who his first followers were, where they travelled and what happened during the last few days of his life. The reader is carried up to the tranquil beauty of the gentle hillside overlooking Lake Galilee, where one can almost feel the breeze and see the vivid colours of the wild flowers at one's feet. Here one can view the world as those first disciples saw it and sense with them the excitement of those early days. Or we can journey with them into Jerusalem for that fatal last week, and live with them through the birth pangs of the Church.

The *second* horizon is that of the writer of the Gospel. As it now stands the Gospel is anonymous, and all we know for certain is that it arose somewhere near to Palestine in about the year 80 AD.

Each of the four Gospels is different. This is because they were written by different people, at different times and in different places. So in Matthew's Gospel we find hints not only about the writer but also about the community to which he or she belonged. In fact, mirrored in the pages of the Gospels we see the reflections of their hopes and fears, their sorrows and joys. In a very real way, that early Christian community was the anvil upon which the teaching of the Gospel was hammered out. Fresh understandings arose as the Christians applied the old sayings of Jesus to new situations. So the Spirit of the risen Jesus continued to address the ongoing life of the Church in the cities of the Mediterranean world.

The *third* horizon is that of our own world. For we, the readers, bring our own dimension into the Gospel. Each of us reads the Gospel from a different perspective, often understanding things in different ways. Time and again we are amazed at the relevance of the Gospel, for although it is nearly two thousand years old it continues to confront and address the issues of today.

This set of studies is designed to help you, the reader, make the Gospel come alive in your own society. First of all, however, we need to know more about the different backgrounds to the Gospel, and in particular the socio-political aspects of Jesus' and Matthew's time.

The first horizon: Palestine in Roman hands

The land of Israel was the crossroad of the ancient world, where east met west, and north met south. It is a land of contrasts, from Hermon in the north, snow-peaked and awesome, to the barrenness of the Negev desert in the south, with low hills evolving into mountainous ridges and rocky passes.

To the west lies the fertile coastal plain, with its series of meandering rivers gently flowing to the Mediterranean or Great Sea. In Galilee the plain penetrates inland in a pleasant valley encircled by mountains, the valley of Esdraelon or Armeggiddon. Here was the breadbasket of Israel, richly fertile. Between the coastal plain and the Jordan valley lie the Central Highlands, a rocky area dividing the country in half from north to south. The lush crops of the fertile plains give way to terraced slopes where groves of olive trees give shelter from the sun to goats and sheep.

The third area is that of the Jordan valley. This is a rift valley, mostly below sea level and including such features as the Sea of Galilee (Lake Kinneret) and the Dead Sea (Salt Sea). Jericho, sited near the northern edge of the Dead Sea, was the chosen winter resort of the wealthy, while Jerusalem, with its cool evening breezes and lofty altitude was the place to be in summer.

Some ten thousand years before Jesus, Palestine was home for the Natufian culture, a community of farmers who lived in caves and mudbrick houses. The first pottery remains found by archaeologists date from the fourth millenium (c4000-3200 BC). The Israelite period begins about 1250 BC, when a spate of small farming villages suddenly blossomed in the Central Highland region. The occupants of these villages were the early Israelites, a new wave of immigrants in a country which had already experienced thousands of years of human history.

As people who knew something of the reality of Egyptian oppression, the early Israelites established a society marked by equality. Slavery was severely restricted, and laws were introduced to protect the weaker members of society, like the orphan or the widow. The story of Deborah (Judges 4 and 5) testifies to the key role played by women in government and in war. Finally, the Jubilee regulations (Leviticus 25) were designed to prevent the wealthy from becoming wealthier at the expense of the poor.

Sadly this equality experienced by the Israelites in the first few centuries under the Judges soon disappeared. The kings of Israel followed the lead of the other ancient Near Eastern kings. Solomon (c950 BC) was not content to live in the simplicity enjoyed by Saul or David. Wishing to emulate the kings of the neighbouring countries, he forced the Israelites to work without pay in his grand building projects. Solomon saw to the creation of a new group of wealthy land owners who benefitted from favours granted by the king. Taxation to support the lavish courts of the kings of Israel, however, became the burden of the poor. Peasant farmers were forced off the land given them by God. Even the Temple of God and its paid priests and prophets were used to exploit the poor. So, in the centuries that followed, God sent other prophets to pour out judgement on the people, and the Kingdoms of Israel (721 BC) and Judah (587 BC) fell to their enemies.

Even after the release from exile in Babylon during the sixth century BC, Israel's experience was largely that of a people in an occupied land. A brief respite occurred in the second century BC when a revolution took place (Maccabees), and for just over half a century Judaea enjoyed political independence. Then it was the turn of the Romans to hold and to occupy Israel. About sixty years later (c 7 BC) Jesus was born.

During the time of Jesus, the land of Palestine was divided into several parts (see map overleaf). Our concern is with two of these regions: Galilee and Judaea. They were separated by a third region called Samaria. The Samaritans were the remnant of the Northern Kingdom of Israel. In the fifth century BC, two Persian officials, Ezra and Nehemiah, had forced the Jews to divorce their Samaritan wives and had forbidden the Samaritans to help rebuild Jerusalem. So in spite of the fact that they were closely related to the Jews of Judaea,

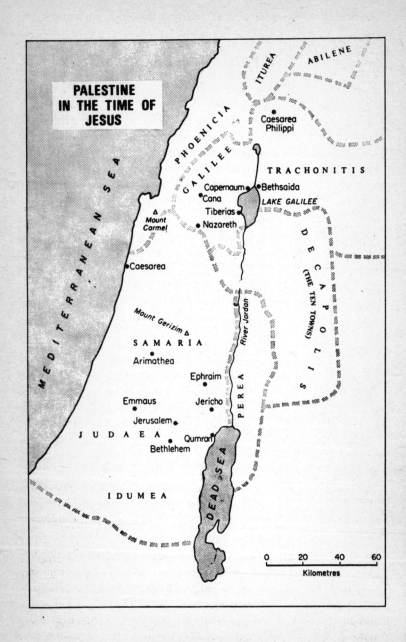

PALESTINE IN THE TIME OF JESUS

the Samaritans were from that time on treated as aliens and apostates.

Galilee was located in the north, sandwiched between Samaria and Syria. The region was different to its southern cousin Judaea in that much of its population was Gentile. This was particularly true for the cities of Galilee, Sepphoris and Tiberius for the rural villages were mainly Jewish. Life was hard for both the farmers and the fisherfolk of Galilee in those times. Although they did not pay taxes directly to Rome, as was the case in Judaea, the burden of taxes imposed by Herod Antipas was very severe. Moreover there were laws which controlled the areas for farming and for fishing, all of which made the life of a Galilean peasant a difficult one.

To make matters worse, tax collectors were hired by the state and expected to earn their wages by charging a percentage over and above the taxation limit. Then there was the matter of tithes and religious taxes (like the half-shekel Temple Tax). What should have been the delight of the people, in giving gifts to God, became instead a terrible burden. One had no choice, for tithes were obligatory. What was even worse was that the country priests often had the offerings they should have received stolen from them by the wealthy priests living in the cities. Some rural clergy actually starved to death.

The cities of Galilee were completely dependent for food on the rural areas. The small farmers found themselves in open competition with the large estates run by absentee landlords. The actual work on these estates was done by peasants who had lost their own farms in the unequal struggle with the elements and their wealthy neighbours. During Jesus' time, more and more of the peasant farmers found themselves separated from the land of their parents, with the sad choice of working on the wealthy estates for a pittance, or seeking their fortune in the cities of Galilee and further afield. Many Jews found that the only way to avoid starvation was to join the Roman army.

The peasants of Galilee had for centuries bartered their crops in exchange for other goods. But when the Romans arrived all that changed. They were forced to sell their crops for cash so that they could pay their taxes. In a bad year, they would have to borrow money, which led to many of them falling deeper and deeper into debt. A not unfamiliar scenario even today.

Galilee was the birth place of several Jewish resistance movements, although life was more congenial there than in either Judaea or Samaria. In the course of Jesus' lifetime, several villages in Galilee experienced the harsh edge of Roman steel during peasant uprisings. These often left hundreds of Jewish people dead in the dusty streets. Indeed, most Jewish families in Galilee would have had relatives who had died or been injured in the course of actions against the Romans. Feelings ran high in Galilee and there was no shortage of reactionaries, ready at a moment's notice to take up arms against Herod and his Roman masters.

Judaea, in contrast to the gentle vista of Galilee, was a place of rocky limestone outcrops, dazzling white in the harsh sunlight, a place of dry grass, frequent famine and harsh living conditions. To the south of Jerusalem a cloud of dust hung in the sky as a permanent reminder of the encroaching desert. In the city itself stood the Temple with its glistening white stones, pure as driven snow, a monument to the might and power of Herod the Great, father of Herod Antipas of Galilee. Most of the people in Jerusalem were directly or indirectly employed by the Temple authorities. Indeed, with the completion of the Temple in 64 AD, some eighteen thousand people were paid off. Scarce wonder that the famous Jewish revolt, culminating in the seige of Masada, started soon afterwards. Moreover the revolt began with the storming and barricading of the Jerusalem Temple by the Jewish freedom fighters.

The courtyard of the Temple was the financial heart of the country. Here pilgrims from every corner of the Mediterranean world gathered for the three major festivals. Money changers accepted coins from all over the Roman empire and, in exchange for a small commission, supplied the Temple shekels necessary to pay the Temple tax and for the purchase of sacrifices. The stalls selling the various animals were located in the same courtyard and one can just imagine the general noise — not forgetting the smells!

There were private and public occasions for visiting Jerusalem, but the largest crowds came during the festivals of Passover, Tabernacles and Sukkoth. During Passover the Roman guard was based in Jerusalem for 'security' reasons. In fact several revolts were caused by Roman soldiers mocking the religious rites of the Jews. The consequences were nearly always the same: thousands of Jews left dead or injured in the streets of their holy city. Yet Passover continued to be a great occasion, for this was the time when the people remembered their bondage in Egypt and the figure of their God as their liberator.

Rule in Judaea from the year 6 AD onward was directly in the hands of the Romans. The Roman presence was headed by a Prefect or Procurator. From the year 25 AD this office was held by Pontius Pilatus, better known as Pilate. Pilate was notorious for his use of force. For example, when he confiscated Temple property to build a new aqueduct for Jerusalem, the people marched in protest. Roman soldiers, in plain clothes and secretly armed, infiltrated the ranks of the marchers and, at a given signal, beat the crowds into submission. Such cruelty led to Pilate's recall to Rome in 35 AD .

Day to day legislation was in the hands of the seventy-two members of the Sanhedrin, mostly Sadducees by birth. They met under the auspices of the High Priest, who belonged to the ruling aristocracy of Jerusalem. All in all there were five families who controlled the fortunes of Judaea, having, through the High Priest, complete control of the Temple, its finances and the religious life of the people. Caiaphas was High Priest during Jesus' time, but it seems that the former High Priest, Annas, continued to wield considerable influence over the families — including his-son-in-law Caiaphas.

The combined economic exploitation of the Sadducees and the military oppression of the Romans was a heavy burden for the people of Judaea and Galilee to bear. As Matthew makes abundantly clear, Jesus addresses himself directly to this situation.

> When he saw the crowds, he had compassion on them, because they were harassed (maltreated) and helpless (wasted or thrown down), like sheep without a shepherd. (Matthew 9:36)

Moreover he brings a message of hope which two thousand years of history cannot diminish.

The second horizon: the church at Antioch

Church tradition over the ages has made Matthew, the disciple of Jesus, the author of this Gospel. However as we have already seen it is an anonymous piece of work. Modern studies of the Gospel reveal that the writer could not have been an eyewitness of Jesus' ministry.

In particular, the writer made extensive use of Mark's Gospel, repeating 600 of Mark's 661 verses. No eyewitness would have needed to do that. All we know for certain is that the writer was a Christian, who compiled the Gospel in about 80 AD (ten years after the Roman destruction of Jerusalem). I shall continue to refer to the writer as Matthew, yet without presupposing the author to be a male. Hence I shall use the double pronoun his/her.

Apart from an early form of Mark's Gospel, Matthew also used a collection of the sayings of Jesus, which scholars call Q. This source is no longer available for us to study. In fact the very existence of Q is a scholarly guess, based on certain parallel texts which exist both in Matthew and Luke, indicating their use of the same source, a source which Mark had not known. As eye-witnesses of Jesus' ministry died, Christians like Matthew saw the need to gather together all the information they could about Jesus, so as to preserve these traditions in a written form. Matthew, in searching for details of the life and teaching of Jesus, obviously came across Q, which he/she recognised as a very early written record of things which Jesus had said.

Using Mark's Gospel as a framework, Matthew inserted a combination of Q material and some material of his/her own. The result was a Gospel twice the length of Mark's. Not that Matthew was just a compiler. No, here was an inspired writer who, in a most creative way, produced a Gospel for the Church.

The birthplace of the Gospel is no longer known, but several scholars have suggested Antioch, a major city in Syria (see the 'scholarly note' at the end of this volume). The apostle Peter was apparently venerated in that place long after his death. Matthew is very interested in Peter, particularly in his role in founding the Church (Matthew 16:16-19). Unlike the communities started by Paul, Matthew's community was strongly Jewish in outlook, with a deep commitment to the Jewish law as interpreted by Jesus. Not that the community did not welcome non-Jews, but all its members, whether Jew or Gentile, were expected to hold to the law of Moses as the basis of Christian ethics. This was not legalism, for Matthew's community was able, through the teaching of Jesus, to rediscover the heart of the Jewish law. Indeed Jesus sums this up for us in Matthew 23:23, when he says:

Woe to you, teachers of the law and Pharisees, you hypocrites! You

give a tenth of your spices - mint, dill and cummin. But you have neglected the more important matters of the law - justice, mercy and faithfulness. You should have practised the latter, without neglecting the
former.

Like the great prophets of the Hebrew Bible, Jesus reminds the
people of God's standards. In contrast to the Jewish teachers of the
time, who used the law to oppress the poor of the land, Jesus is represented by Matthew as invoking the spirit of the law to create a new
sense of freedom. How this is achieved will become clearer later in
this book.

Matthew's community is a community under persecution. The
Christians are persecuted by both Jews (Matthew 5:12) and Romans.
After the destruction of Jerusalem in 70 AD, the Jewish rabbis reorga-
nised the Judaism of the day. The result was that only orthodox
Pharisaism was considered acceptable, and all other forms of
Judaism were rejected. Many Jews found themselves cut off from
their religious moorings. The Matthean community reached out to
these people with open arms, offering them a social and religious
identity within a new Israel. But in the process of reaching out,
Matthew's community aroused the anger of the orthodox Pharisees,
and many Christians suffered as a result.

The long years of Roman persecution were only beginning when
Matthew wrote his/her Gospel. In the years which followed thousands of Christians were to die for their faith. Matthew attempts to
warn them of the coming time.

The social class of the Matthean community was varied. The majority
would have been freedpersons (people who were once slaves). The
rest of the community consisted of free people, largely middle class,
along with a few slaves. Living within a city like Antioch the community would have been exposed to the harsh realities of Roman rule
and to the poverty which even to today is endemic in the Middle East.

Matthew's Gospel contains advice on surviving persecution and on
coping with oppression. It is a Gospel about God's presence as evident in the name given to Jesus: Immanuel — God is with us, even in
our suffering.

The third horizon: the church today

The Gospel of Matthew continues to address the context of the church today, in our time. The risen Lord towers above the pages of the Gospel and his authority echoes through the portals of the years. The experiences faced by Matthew's community are our experiences, and we in turn kneel at the feet of the Master and hear him speak his new word to our own generation. The Prophet of Galilee still speaks with a disquieting tone, and the standards of his community rule seem as unattainable as ever.

As we use our own social context to interpret the Gospel, as we read the pages against the backdrop of our own time, as we listen to the voices of the suffering communities about us, we find a third horizon. Beyond the world of Jesus, and the oppression of the Romans. Beyond the world of Matthew and the fear of Roman or Jewish persecution. Beyond both these worlds is the world in which we live, and work and worship.

The Gospel of Matthew is nothing, if it does not speak to our own age, if it does not address the questions of our time. But how can it? How can a book written two thousand years ago possibly speak to the nuclear age, the world of sophisticated technology, to people suffering under the oppression of ideologies like 'apartheid'? Yet it does! Perhaps because there are some things which never change. To quote the words of that strange Hebrew philosopher, Koheleth:

> Again I looked and saw all the oppression that was taking place under the sun: I saw the tears of the oppressed - and they have no comforter; power was on the side of their oppressors - but they had no comforter.
> (Ecclesiastes 4:1)

As we walk the paths of the Gospel we shall marvel again and again at the way in which Matthew's Gospel does indeed offer insights into contemporary issues. For people everywhere with firsthand experience of oppression and injustice, the Gospel carries a message of hope unequalled by all but the Gospel of John. In its simplest form it expresses the assurance of PRESENCE, from the birth of Immanuel (God with us) to the promise of Jesus to his disciples in chapter 28: 'Lo I am always with you even to the end of the age'. The presence of the risen Lord meets the reader at every turn.

There is a more awesome side to the Gospel. Its vivid expectation of the return of Jesus burns like a flame against the darkness of the present age. Yes, there will come a time when Jesus will return to judge not only the world but also his Church and to separate out the chaff from the wheat, the bad from the good. For those people whose ears burn with the lies of the false prophets of our present age, where churches are platforms for the gods of materialism and oppression, the judgement cannot come soon enough.

Matthew is the Gospel for the Church. It brings good news for the poor and judgement for the wicked. It is a Gospel which divides like a two-edged sword. If even a little of the power of that word comes through in this brief commentary, I will have achieved my goal.

Bible Studies: Matthew's Portrait of Jesus

Jesus: King, Prophet and Son of God

Three great themes come together in Matthew's Gospel, namely Jesus as a King like David, Jesus as a Teacher and Prophet like Moses and Jesus as the Son of God. We shall study each in turn, for each has something different to say to our present day context.

JESUS AS KING

The Gospel opens with a presentation of the birth of Jesus and one is immediately struck by the deliberate connection with King David. In the mention of Bethlehem and the later visit of the wise men bearing royal gifts, we have clear signs of the royal nature of Jesus. Truly this is the birth of a king.

Later in the Gospel, Jesus is contrasted with Solomon. '. . . and now one greater than Solomon is here' (12:42). In what way is Jesus greater than Solomon, the reader might enquire? Two features of the tradition surrounding Solomon suggest an answer. In the first place Solomon shares two titles in common with Jesus, namely Son of David (Matthew 12:23) and Son of God (Matthew 16:16 *cf* 2 Samuel 7:14). But for Matthew, Jesus is not just a Messiah like David or Solomon, he is a divine figure. This is evident at several places in the Gospel, but most explicitly in the action of the disciples as they worship Jesus (Matthew 14:33 and 28:17). So Jesus is uniquely the Son of David and the Son of God and hence superior to all other claimants to these titles.

Secondly, Solomon was considered to have been a great magician and exorcist. This tradition was not found in the Hebrew Bible, but was well known during the time of Jesus. Hence Jesus' actions would have reminded the people of Solomon. When he casts out demons, they enquire whether this is the Son of David, meaning Solomon (12:23). This leads Jesus to state that he casts out demons by the power of the Spirit (12:28) and to his conclusion that he is greater than Solomon (12:42). This is no magician like Solomon, this is God's chosen agent, empowered and equipped with the Holy Spirit.

The following four studies in Matthew show us further details of Matthew's picture of Jesus the King.

In the studies I will refer to 'our group' or to 'the leader'. That is because these Bible Studies have grown out of small group discussions from within the South African context. The issues faced, however, are universal and so we believe that the studies will speak to people all over the world. As we have used the passages in Matthew's Gospel to speak to our own situation, so you, the reader, will be given the opportunity to do the same.

We encourage you to follow the steps which we used in our own studies, to discuss the same issues and to answer the same questions. But because your context may be different to ours we urge that in preparing for each study, you look for parallels within your own social and political context. Think and talk about the issues faced in your own society, and use the Gospel to find solutions. Our own excitement at seeing the Gospel 'come alive' was quite unforgettable. For too long the Bible has been restricted to the religious domain, imprisoned in church buildings and divorced from the market-place of life.

1. The Birth of the King

Matthew 1:18 - 25

Matthew's picture of Jesus as a king is full of surprises. Unfortunately our familiarity with the stories often deadens the impact. So we will need to try hard to recapture the impression these stories must have had on the people of Matthew's own time.

In our group, to help the participants feel more at ease, we decided to start this study with an icebreaker. We began by exchanging childhood memories of Christmas, allowing each person two minutes for their story. Then the group leader read the passage from Matthew 1. We tried to imagine what Mary or Joseph felt, so as to discover the real people behind the Christmas card imagery.

> 18 **This is how the birth of Jesus Christ came about. His mother Mary was pledged to be married to Joseph, but before they came together, she was found to be with child through the Holy Spirit.**
>
> 19 **Because Joseph her husband was a righteous man and did not want to expose her to public disgrace, he had in mind to divorce her quietly.**
>
> 20 **But after he had considered this, an angel of the Lord appeared to him in a dream and said, 'Joseph son of David, be not afraid to take Mary home as your wife, because what is conceived in her is from the Holy Spirit.**
>
> 21 **She will give birth to a son, and you are to give him the name Jesus, because he will save his people from their sins.'**
>
> 22 **All this took place to fulfill what the Lord had said through the prophet:**
>
> 23 **The virgin will be with child and will give birth to a son, and they will call him Immanuel' — which means, 'God with us.'**
>
> 24 **When Joseph woke up, he did what the angel of the Lord had commanded him and took Mary home as his wife.**
>
> 25 **But he had no union with her until she gave birth to a son. And he gave him the name Jesus.**
>
> *Matthew 1:18-25*

After a few minutes of discussion we worked through the notes on the text together. Both for this session and for future sessions you might prefer to have someone prepare their own summary of the notes, rather than simply reading aloud what is printed below. Alternatively, you might have the group take turns to read a verse from Matthew followed by the notes on that verse. Perhaps you could even take a few verses at a time in this way.

Notes on the text

Background

The Gospel of Matthew, like Luke, begins with an account of Jesus' birth. First, the evangelist gives us details of Jesus' genealogy, selecting names from the Old Testament. Matthew's list contains three times fourteen generations. This was intentional. Matthew is using the list as a cipher: Hebrew has no numerals — instead, certain letters have numerical value. For example, D is 4 and the Vuv (v) is 6. Vowels are left out of Biblical Hebrew so the 'value' of the word David (D_v_d) is $4 + 6 + 4$ which equals 14. Matthew's list of three times fourteen generations is thus spelling out the name of King David three times over. In doing this Matthew gives Jesus a threefold affirmation for his claim to be the royal messiah — the Christ.

The writer then turns his/her attention to the actual events of the birth, commencing with the marriage of Mary and Joseph. In Jewish tradition at that time, a marriage was a combination of two legal actions. The first of these was the taking of the marriage vows, with the promising of the woman and man for marriage to each other. This is the equivalent of certain African ceremonies, where the families of the couple meet together to decide the legal terms of the marriage. In Galilee the marriage could then be sexually consummated, but in Judaea this was not so. However, in both cases the couple would reside apart for about a year. At the end of this period, the marriage feast took place. First the woman was conducted to the bridegroom's home, to be followed later that evening by the bridegroom himself returning from his bachelor's party. Then the guests arrived and the celebrations began in earnest.

Text

Verse 18 indicates that Mary and Joseph were in the first stage of their marriage and had not yet 'come together'. The Greek word which is translated 'betrothed' simply means married, for already at that early stage the couple would be legally bound in marriage and to sever the relationship required a writ of divorce. So Matthew calls them husband and wife (verse 19). The reader, having been prepared by the genealogy to expect the birth of a royal child, now receives a jolt. Mary is pregnant already and it is before she and Joseph have consummated their marriage, so Joseph cannot be the father.

Matthew assures the reader that the pregnancy is 'of the Holy Spirit' which means that it was in accordance with the will of God and not that the Holy Spirit was an active male partner in the process. So far there is no indication that this pregnancy is any different from any other.

Verse 19 addresses the dilemma of Joseph. We are not told how Mary felt. Joseph is a follower of traditional Jewish teaching, a pious and a just person. On account of his religious convictions or perhaps in spite of them, he decides to disobey the tradition and to divorce Mary in as quiet a way as possible. The custom of the day called for a public action, rather like the practice of 'tarring and feathering' someone.

In verse 20 an angel of the Lord intervenes to tell Joseph that Mary's pregnancy is completely in line with the will of God. By calling Joseph son of David, we, the readers, are reminded again of the royal nature of the event. Once more the reader learns that it is 'of the Holy Spirit'.

Mary will bear a son, to be named Jesus. Jeshua, the Hebrew for Jesus, means 'God is my helper'. We learn that Jesus 'will save (hoshea) his people from their sins'. There is a deliberate pun upon the name Jesus and the verb 'to save'. Although meaning different things, the terms were often linked together and shared a similar sound. The idea of saving people from their sins meant more than the simple action of securing God's forgiveness on their behalf. The Hebrew Bible is full of instances where God's act of salvation goes beyond forgiveness to include a setting free of people from the results of sin in society. In Palestine in the first century, saving people from their sins included, of necessity, putting an end to their oppression. So Matthew retains the hope that with the return of Jesus in triumph, oppression will end.

Verse 22 looks back to the greatest foreteller of the messianic age, namely the prophet Isaiah. Matthew's concern with the teaching of the new Jewish Christians is evident in the constant reference, in the form of allusions or actual quotations, to the Hebrew Bible. Passionately he/she believes that the promises of God are now being actualised.

Now, in verse 23, the evangelist quotes Isaiah from the Greek translation of the Hebrew Bible, called today the Septuagint. This translation was popular with both the Greek-speaking Jews of the diaspora (the name given to Jews who live outside Palestine) and the early Christians. The passage Matthew refers to is Isaiah 7:14:

> Therefore the Lord himself will give you a sign: The virgin will be with child and will give birth to a son and will call him Immanuel.

By using the Greek translation, Matthew is able to introduce the idea of a 'virgin' birth — in contrast to the Hebrew Old Testament where the term was *alma* meaning 'young woman'. However, very few Jews of Matthew's time would have known that fact nor would they have been perturbed by such selective use of texts.

Up to this point the reader would have had no idea that the birth of Jesus was somehow supernatural. Matthew's readers would have presumed that Mary had had a lover, but that the affair had nevertheless been a part of God's plan. Now Matthew introduces a new dimension as, by means of the quotation, he/she allows the reader to conclude that Jesus was born of a virgin. Whether Mary's community believed that this was a virgin birth we will never know. Certainly there is good reason to believe that Mary would have carried the hurt of the accusation of adultery for at least a part of her life.

The title given to the child of Isaiah's vision is Immanuel. Jesus never receives this as his name but the impact of the message remains with the reader. Here already, in a wonderful way, Matthew is confirming for the community the presence of God in their midst. God has come to be with these people in a new and revolutionary way.

Verses 24 and 25 conclude the section, and we see Joseph responding to the dream. He accordingly brings to pass the second part of the marriage and, when Jesus is born, he assumes the legal role of the father by naming Jesus.

Unlike Luke, Matthew leaves one with the impression that Mary and Joseph were natives of Bethlehem (2:22-24), who chose to immigrate to Nazareth because of the tyranny of Archelaus, ruler of Judaea after Herod the Great. The coming of the Magi (wise people) from the east (Mesopotamia) is designed to draw attention to Jesus' universal kingship. His brief sojourn in Egypt reminds us of Moses, suggesting that Jesus fulfils the promise of Deuteronomy 18:18 as the Second Moses. Already we see several themes coming together. Jesus as a king like David and as a prophet like Moses comes onto the stage. So the reader is prepared for the functions which Jesus will fulfil. He will become the great intrepreter of the Law and one day he will reign as the universal king.

Discussion
After discussing some of the questions coming out of the passage, we shared our thoughts about the pain that Mary may have experienced. For many people she would have been seen as a single mother. Together we read the reflection.

Reflection

Like a surgeon's lance the pain of rejection cut deep inside her. She turned her face to the wall so she no longer saw the crib. Put her hands to her ears to block the sound of the child's happy play. Why her? What had she done to deserve this fate? Why was it that in a society that spoke about free love, she should be the one to pay the cost? Her mirror gave her no reply, but silently mocked her anguished face that yet bore traces of her childhood. It was not the anger of her parents, or the coldness of her lover that hurt her most. No, it was the expressions on the faces of the people she half-knew, the look of pity and embarrassment, as if she was some kind of alien who had given birth to an alien child. She felt exposed, stripped of her pride, naked in a world of people cloaked by their sense of self-righteousness. She was God's humourless jest, a caricature of the incarnation.

Wisely the group leader steered the discussion away from a debate on the virgin birth, towards an appreciation of God's wisdom. God used the birth of Jesus to bring home a deep sense of caring for people who suffer the ostracism of society. We spent time thinking about people we knew who suffered in this way. We then closed in prayer, with a focus on these people.

2. The Kingdom of the King

Matthew 5:1-12

At the beginning of the second study our group divided into pairs, and each told the other briefly about ourselves and how we perceived the role of the church in our society. After ten minutes the leader called us together and asked us whether the message of the local church could be called 'good news'. Was it good news for people outside of that church? Was it good news for the poor? Your leader might like to add questions of his/her own.

Our group was rather divided, and we began to see how our own class position and place in society affected our opinions. For those who were in daily contact with some form of oppression, the church which did not address itself to that context was largely irrelevant. For those whose major concern was keeping up a particular social status, the spirituality of the church was primary. After pointing out these differences one of the group then summarised the section on the social situation in Palestine for the rest of us (see p. 12 above). Then together we worked through the passage and the notes.

¹ Now when he saw the crowds, he went up on a
mountainside and sat down. His disciples came to him,
² and he began to teach them, saying:
³ 'Blessed are the poor in spirit,
for theirs is the kingdom of heaven.
⁴ Blessed are those who mourn,
for they will be comforted.
⁵ Blessed are the meek,
for they will inherit the earth.
⁶ Blessed are those who hunger and thirst for righteousness,
for they will be filled.
⁷ Blessed are the merciful,
for they will be shown mercy.
⁸ Blessed are the pure in heart,
for they will see God.
⁹ Blessed are the peacemakers,
for they will be called sons of God.
¹⁰ Blessed are those who are persecuted because of righteousness,
for theirs is the kingdom of heaven.
¹¹ Blessed are you when people insult you, persecute you and falsely say all kinds of evil against you because of me.
¹² Rejoice and be glad, because great is your reward in heaven, for in the same way they persecuted the prophets who were before you.

Matthew 5:1-12

Notes on the text

Background

We come now to the greatest collection of the teachings of Jesus found in any of the Gospels. We call it the Sermon on the Mount, but clearly it is a series of sermons, or parts of sermons, grouped together by Matthew for his or her own teaching purposes. Luke has similar material scattered throughout his whole Gospel, and we shall refer to Luke's version several times.

The Sermon on the Mount deals with the basic issues of living as a Christian in a secular society. Oppression, hatred, immorality, divorce, revenge and the practice of Christian charity are just some of the issues which are dealt with by the author. The sermon opens with a series of blessings (5:1-12) and ends with a series of warnings (7:1,15,21 and 26-27). This pattern is similar to the Book of the Law (Deuteronomy) which suggests that Matthew intends to draw a parallel between Jesus and Moses — both revealers of the commandments of God. So we shall return to the sermon when we consider Jesus as the Prophet like Moses. For the moment we shall consider the opening blessings as a way of understanding something about the kingdom of the King.

Jesus' sermon addresses the unspoken question of the crowds of his own time and of course of Matthew's audience. The question is, 'How does Jesus' religious teaching affect our work-a-day lives?' For the common people of Galilee, many of whom had lost relatives at the hands of the Romans or Herod's soldiers, and who were daily witnesses to the cruelty of these same soldiers, the question would have been couched in terms of their continual experience of oppression and misery. For Matthew's audience, living on the brink of one of the worst periods of persecution in living memory, the question was tinged with fear for the future. One and all longed for a new world, free from the heavy burden of taxation and Roman domination.

Jesus answers their question as he propounds a lifestyle designed to cope with the rigours of both oppression and persecution. But he begins with a series of breathtaking statements about the kingdom of God and the way in which that kingdom will reverse the standards of the present world order. For a brief moment the doors of the kingdom stand ajar and we catch a glimpse of the world inside. In a revolutionary way, Jesus overthrows the burdens created by the Pharisaic interpretation of the Law, and imposed by them upon the class of people called the 'People of the Land'. A massive group of people were so described, indeed the bulk of the peasantry and urban poor were in this class. Lacking proper education they were unable to read or study the Law and so were seen to be unworthy of being taught it. Victims of the social structure, they were barred from the Pharisees' vision of God's kingdom. They were doomed to be outside God's kingdom because they lacked the minimum educational qualifications and the attendant financial advantages.

Sidney Holo

Text

In direct response to such teaching Jesus says, 'Blessed (happy) are the poor in spirit, for theirs is the kingdom of heaven' (5:3). In other words, the very people whom the Pharisees declare to be beyond the pale, will be those who inherit the kingdom of God. This was really good news for the poor, not only of Jesus' time but also of Matthew's own time, when the teaching of the Pharisees was in the process of becoming the accepted teaching of mainstream Judaism. Here was a complete reversal of such teaching.

Luke has simply 'Blessed are you who are poor, for yours is the kingdom of God' (6:20). Matthew's inclusion of the words 'in spirit' has led some people to suggest that Matthew has in mind some other category of people apart from the literal poor, as in Luke. Perhaps he/she intends the 'spiritually poor'? If by spiritually poor one means a poverty of spiritual riches, one is soon aware that such a reading is simply not tenable: Jesus promotes spiritual riches, not spiritual poverty (Matthew 6:20 and 13:45,52).

Perhaps Jesus intends a blessing upon those who know their own spiritual poverty and honestly seek for God's salvation? I feel that this view must also be rejected. First of all, Matthew could have said this, had he/she wanted that sense to become clear, by simply adding the words 'know themselves to be'. This is not done, and we have no right to read the text as if those words were present.

So we come back to the sense closest to Luke's version, namely that the poor in spirit are also those who are poor in economic terms. The underlying Hebrew phrase implies someone who is both poor and lacking in spirit, that is, someone who has been robbed of material means and of dignity. We may imagine a collection of poor people, eyes dull with lack of emotion. Poor and without spirit, they are the tired victims of a cruel society.

These people, the poor of spirit, are the one's to whom Jesus promises the kingdom of his Father. The paradoxical nature of this interpretation is the very sign of its authenticity. The saying is designed to be shocking.

Verse 4 is similar. 'Blessed are those who mourn, for they shall be comforted'. We know that the death of someone close to us is traumatic, but so often people in the Western world forget that they have been carefully cushioned against the worst side of death's face. The graveyards of the squatter camps, the children dying in the streets are much closer to the reality of Jesus' time than the clinical cleanliness of the funeral parlour. To the people of Jesus' time, with a life expectation of only twenty-five years, death was a constant companion. Not the quiet death of a hospital ward — the privilege of the well to do — but the brutal and violent death of the poor. Jesus speaks into the context of all who have known the pain of people dying about them. Be glad when you mourn, for God will comfort you. Like the great poet Job, Jesus affirms that God is with us in **our** suffering. The time will come when the dispossessed will inherit the kingdom and when the people who now mourn will find that God has wiped away their tears.

Verse 5 confirms the previous verses and is perhaps the most striking. 'Blessed are the meek, for they shall inherit the earth'. Traditionally the word meek has been taken to imply the humble or self-effacing. The opposite would then be those who are proud and arrogant. However, this interpretation ignores the fact that Jesus is quoting scripture here, namely Psalm 37:11. The word rendered as meek is *oni* or poor, and the Psalm clearly indicates that it is the literal poor who are intended. Jesus uses the Psalm to stress that it is not the present rich rulers but the poor people who will be the ones to inherit 'the land', that is the land of Israel, or alternatively God's kingdom, which was expected to become evident within the borders of the historical Israel.

The first three beatitudes might then be paraphrased as follows:

> Happy are those who are poor and stripped even of their spirit, for they will possess God's kingdom.
> Happy are those for whom brutal death is a constant companion, for God shall comfort them.
> Happy are those who have been oppressed, for they shall inherit God's land.

The remainder of the Beatitudes addresses more directly Matthew's own time, with a particular concern for the experience of religious and social persecution, and for the living out of the Christian life. This is not to say that the Matthean community did not identify also with the first three blessings. The Jewish people of the Dead Sea Community, who had voluntarily given up their riches in order to share their wealth with the rest of their community, identified themselves with the poor of Psalm 37:11. These Jewish monastics believed that because of their ultra-religious way of life, God would one day give the land of Israel to their community. Instead, the Roman soldiers destroyed their community. In a very different way Matthew's community would have understood all the blessings to relate to them, and the church through the ages has simply continued in their steps. What I have attempted to do is to show why Matthew's presentation of the kingdom was good news for his/her first hearers. The kingdom of the King is first of all for those who have nothing and who suffer most.

Discussion

There were several questions and comments, particularly about the poor in spirit. We discussed these and then spent a little while thinking about the social, political and spiritual impact of Jesus for his time. Then we read the reflection.

Reflection

The little boy trundled his wire wheel down the dusty road, lost in the oblivion of his game, when a shot rang out. He crashed in a bloody, crumpled heap while the wheel rolled on. Silence fell and the eyes of the people looked around for the killer. Was it aimed or accidental, fired by friend or fired by foe? One man moved. Old and tired, the grandfather of the boy stumbled down the way the boy had played. He bent and picked up the child, holding him close as he had done so many times before. Symbol of parents throughout the ages, from the famines of Ethiopia to the middle-eastern refugee camps, his eyes searched the heavens for an answer. Framed against the sky he lifted the child above his head and cried, 'How many children have to die, before you set my people free?'

The reflection sparked off quite a heated discussion on the local situation in the country. The leader ended the session shortly after this even though the group was so clearly divided. A mood of hopelessness fell upon the group and a feeling of sadness and frustration.

3. The Parables of the King

Matthew 25:31-46

We began by calling to mind aspects of the previous two studies. This was done through the medium of a game. The leader said a word (eg food, fun) and each person in the group would in turn say the first thing which came into his/her head (eg hamburger, football). After some minutes of laughter and fun, the leader changed the tone and said 'Jesus, the King'. Each of us responded in a sentence or word to the cue. The leader noted these down and after the circle was completed and we had all had our turn, these became the basis for a brief discussion. The group leader then produced a prepared chart entitled Jesus the King, (made by copying one of the drawings from this book), and we each added our phrase or word to the chart. Thus we made up a word picture of Matthew's presentation of King Jesus.

We began to understand a little of the unusual nature of this king. Born not in a palace but in a hovel, of a woman perceived by many to be a sinner, and whose kingdom was shaped for the outcasts of society. The passionate concern of God for the suffering and oppressed began to shine through this picture. Matthew's portrait of the king was in itself a theological statement about God's deep concern for all people — but especially for those forced to live on the fringes of our societies.

We read together the passage, and the notes, followed by a brief discussion on its implications for ourselves.

31 'When the Son of Man comes in his glory, and all the angels with him, he will sit on his throne in heavenly glory.

32 All the nations will be gathered before him, and he will separate the people one from another as a shepherd separates the sheep from the goats.

33 He will put the sheep on his right and the goats on his left.

34 Then the King will say to those on his right, "Come, you who are blessed by my Father; take your inheritance, the kingdom prepared for you since the creation of the world.

35 For I was hungry and you gave me something to eat, I was thirsty and you gave me something to drink, I was a stranger and you invited me in,

³⁶ I needed clothes and you clothed me, I was sick and you looked after me, I was in prison and you came to visit me."

³⁷ Then the righteous will answer him, "Lord, when did we see you hungry and feed you, or thirsty and give you something to drink?

³⁸ When did we see you a stranger and invite you in, or needing clothes and clothe you?

³⁹ When did we see you sick or in prison and go to visit you?"

⁴⁰ The King will reply, "I tell you the truth, whatever you did for one of the least of these brothers of mine, you did for me."

⁴¹ Then he will say to those on his left, "Depart from me, you who are cursed, into the eternal fire prepared for the devil and his angels.

⁴² For I was hungry and you gave me nothing to eat, I was thirsty and you gave me nothing to drink,

⁴³ I was a stranger and you did not invite me in, I needed clothes and you did not clothe me, I was sick and in prison and you did not look after me."

⁴⁴ They also will answer, "Lord, when did we see you hungry or thirsty or a stranger or needing clothes or sick or in prison, and did not help you?"

⁴⁵ He will reply, "I tell you the truth, whatever you did not do for one of the least of these, you did not do for me."

⁴⁶ Then they will go away to eternal punishment, but the righteous to eternal life.'

Matthew 25:31-46

Notes on the text

Background

Matthew recounts a number of the parables of Jesus. The chief characters vary, but in those parables where God is represented, it is usually as a landowner or as a king. So we have the two stories about owners of vineyards (Matthew 20:1-16 and 21:33-41) and a tale about a king who invites guests to his banquet (Matthew 22:2-14). Jesus is represented in various ways. For example, he is a bridegroom (Matthew 25:1-12), a master of servants (Matthew 25:14-30) and a king (Matthew 25:31-46). In each of these parables, and indeed in earlier parables like the sower (Matthew 13:18-23), the presence of Jesus heralds judgement upon humanity. In each of the four examples cited two groups of people are present, the righteous and the unrighteous and Jesus is the judge between the two.

We are reminded here of the expectation found in the Hebrew Bible of the messianic king, who would come as the vice-regent of God to judge the world in justice and righteousness. For example, Isaiah 11:4 reads:

> But with righteousness he will judge (for) the needy, with justice he will give decisions for (in favour of) the poor of the earth.

Jesus, as the messianic king, comes to judge the world. He comes to re-orientate the world to the standards of God. Hence he declares that 'the first shall be last and the last shall be first' (Matthew 19:30). The good news for the poor will be made manifest in the coming kingdom when Jesus pours out his judgement upon the forces of evil. How the hearts of the people of Jesus' time must have filled with joy at this news.

In Matthew's time the news was no less glorious, but it also carried a sense of warning. At the beginning of the Church, when most Christians were deeply committed to the cause of Christ, there was little space for distinction between one person and another. But as the Church grew, so it became evident that not everyone who claimed the name of Jesus was as committed as those first followers. Already by the time of the writing of Matthew's Gospel (c 80 AD) there is the problem of apathetic Christians and divided congregations. So Matthew groups several parables together in chapter 25 as a warning to the people of his/her community, that not all those who start off on the Christian path will be accepted into the heavenly kingdom of Christ. God through Jesus will judge not only the world, but the very Church itself.

The following parable brings this teaching out with absolute clarity. Christians are to live out their faith or they will face the wrath of God. Blind allegiance to an overly literal understanding of Paul's teaching on justification by faith has led some Christians (of the post-reformation era) to ignore both this parable and the words of James, brother of Jesus, who wrote that:

> Faith without works is dead. *(James 2:17)*

So let us consider Matthew's portrait of Jesus, the royal judge of both the world and the Christian community.

Text

Matthew commences (25:31) with a description of Jesus as the Son of Man coming in glory to take up his throne in the kingdom of God. We are reminded of the vivid picture in Daniel 7:13-14 in which the one like a human being (like a son of man, or more accurately like a child of humanity), receives the power, the glory and the kingdom from the hand of God. Matthew verse 32 sets out the scene with Jesus separating the righteous from the unrighteous, like a shepherd dividing sheep and goats.

Jesus then describes the Child of Humanity/Son of Man taking up his position facing the two groups. For those on his right he is defender, for those on his left he is the prosecutor (cf Zechariah 3:1 where Satan is in the position of accuser). Verse 34 adds a new dimension by switching from the title Son of Man, to King, although the mention of the throne in verse 31 had already prepared us for this.

The King invites 'the sheep' to inherit the kingdom (verse 34) and explains their status as blessed. These are the ones who fed him when he was hungry, gave him drink when he was thirsty and invited him in when he was a stranger. They clothed him when naked, visited him when sick, and came to his aid (a better reading than visited) when he was in prison (verses 35 and 36). The sheep, now identified explicitly as the righteous, ask how this can be, since they do not recall such acts of kindness by themselves to the King (verses 37-39). The response of the King is an astonishing one. 'Truly I say to you, to the extent that you did it to one of these brothers (or sisters) of mine, even the least of them, you did it to me' (verse 40).

The reverse fate befalls the unrighteous 'goats' and they find that they are sent away to eternal punishment (verse 46) for not showing kindness to the least of their fellow humans, and so indirectly, to the King.

This powerful parable speaks volumes into the context of any community where people suffer without the comfort of friends to care for them. These people, as envisaged in the parable, are not middle class prodigals but the lowest class of people, the destitute. Jesus must have known them in his own community, Matthew knew them in his/her Christian community and we meet them at every corner of the road. What should our response be? Jesus' word cuts through the claims of people to be true believers, when their lives deny that statement and bear mute testimony to their lack of caring and concern.

The Messiah, described in Isaiah 11, is a judge who will act on behalf of the poor and suffering. He will be their redeemer and their saviour.

But that is not all, for he will, according to this parable, judge people according to the way in which they treat their fellow human beings. This bias towards the defenceless has already been made clear in the opening three beatitudes, which we studied earlier. We are reminded of the great Old Testament picture of God as the *Go-el* or Redeemer of the poor (Proverbs 23:10-11). Of all the pictures in the Hebrew Bible, the image of God as the protector of the orphan and the widow (Psalm 68:5) towers above the others. There is no doubt that of all the categories in human society, none are closer to the heart of God than those who have no human defender, the powerless and the down-trodden.

God remains the Redeemer of the defenceless, we cannot take away that responsibility. The message of the incarnation of Jesus openly declares God's abhorrence of injustice and human suffering. Already, through the judgement initiated in the cross of Jesus, God has acted in an irreversible fashion on behalf of all those who suffer at the hands of others. This parable carries that action to its logical conclusion. As Jesus has suffered to redeem all humanity — particularly those whose lives are filled with misery — so we as his followers are called to carry forward that same message. In our lives and in our actions we are to be the protector of those who have no protector, to be the guardian of the orphan and the defender of the widow.

Discussion

In our discussion we kept the focus on the underlying sense of God's care for those people who are so often the victims of our societies. For the well to do, the parable was to motivate deeds of kindness, but for the poor it spoke aloud of God's concern. In closing we read the reflection and we listed some ways in which we might apply the lesson of the parable to our own lives.

Reflection

The neon lights painted coloured lines in the wetness of the city streets. Cars hummed by like forgotten tubas in the mindless orchestra of the city. Theatre doors disgorged their clientele onto the busy streets and pavements, where they joined the marching crowds. Like puppets controlled by a master puppeteer they move in unison. Then suddenly, like a tragic actor clothed in the pseudo-smartness of a suit too big, he came. His manners bespoke his coun-

try origin, while his wide-eyed innocence told of his recent arrival in the city. Looking up to unseeing faces, calling out to stopped-up ears, reaching out to unfeeling hands, he came. He had not lived long enough to learn the truth about the city. He did not yet realise that the god of the city had blinded the eyes of the people so they could no longer see, deafened them by his cacophany so they could no longer hear, crushed them in his mills so that they could no longer feel.

There was no further discussion, but we used some of the suggestions of the reflection in the time of prayer. You might prefer to explore the meaning of the reflection for your own situation. How does urbanization effect people in your society? What can the Church do to help? At the end of the study our group was more unified than it had been before, although there were still differences of opinion.

4. The Death of the King

Matthew 27:27-29,35-38, 50-51

As we came together for the fourth time, we realised that there were still many differences between us which we needed to talk out. Undoubtedly the picture of Matthew's King was creating some differences of opinion. We found that time and again we were guilty of trying to force Jesus into our own peculiar mould. Yet we longed to be free of this and able to take a long and objective look at the Matthean Jesus.

We started the study by looking at Isaiah 53:1-8. We each read a verse and then commented briefly on what we had read. The group leader then introduced a discussion on the idea of vicarious suffering (that is, suffering on behalf of other people). We used examples which were familiar to us. In your context, you might refer to actual incidents and people known to you. What effect did the suffering have? Then we read the reflection.

Reflection
Like Odysseus, the fabled Greek adventurer, he came to claim the kingdom for his own. Without his royal robes, his crown and mighty

army, no one realised who he was. Defenceless, he rode through the city gates to the music of other people praying for a coming king. Unrecognised he stood among his own people. Their pain was his pain, their oppression was his oppression, and their suffering was his suffering. When he challenged the tyrannical monster that held them captive, the people did not understand. Confused by the tyrant's smiling ways, they looked elsewhere for the cause of their sorrow.

The duel began, and the king and the monster warred against each other, to the consternation of the people. 'There is no monster here,' they cried, 'only a friendly apparition. If you would really set us free, fight those soldiers in the streets.' It seemed that only the king could see that the soldiers and the monster danced to the same tune.

At last the king snatched away the tyrant's smiling mask to expose the naked hatred and lust for power that lay beneath. For a brief moment truth reigned supreme before the clouds of deceit returned. As a signpost for the people the king placed his sword, a cross, to divide the way between sacrificial love and materialistic lust, between God and Mammon. And on that post he hung the monster's mask, so that those who stood in the shadow of the cross might see and understand.

After we had silently thought through the allegory, we read the following passage from Matthew.

27 The governor's soldiers took Jesus into the Praetorium and gathered the whole company of soldiers around him.

28 They stripped him and put a scarlet robe on him,

29 and then wove a crown of thorns and set it on his head. They put a staff in his right hand and knelt in front of him and mocked him. 'Hail, King of the Jews!' they said.

35 When they had crucified him, they divided up his clothes by casting lots.

36 And sitting down, they kept watch over him there.

37 Above his head they placed the written charge against him: THIS IS JESUS, THE KING OF THE JEWS.

38 Two robbers were crucified with him, one on his right and one on his left.

50 And when Jesus had cried out again in a loud voice, he gave up his spirit.

⁵¹ At that moment the curtain of the temple was torn in two from top to bottom. The earth shook and the rocks split.

Matthew 27:27-29, 35-38, 50-51

We related the allegory to the Bible passage by reflecting on the following questions. Who was the hero? What was the duel? Who was the monster? Why did the people want the hero to fight the soldiers in the street? Why did they not understand that the monster was the real threat? Our answers were varied and we were encouraged to use our imagination. We then turned to the notes.

Notes on the text

Background

Matthew, like the other Gospel writers, devotes a great deal of space to the last few days of the life of Jesus. We read the stirring details of the procession into Jerusalem. Matthew likens Jesus to the king depicted in Zechariah 9:9 ('humble' or, better, 'poor' and 'riding on an ass'). We read too of Jesus' cleansing of the Temple, the action which leads inevitably to his death. Why was this so? The answer may be found in a comparison between the procession of Jesus and the victory procession of the Jewish freedom fighters (the Maccabees).

In December 164 BC the Maccabees cleansed the Temple after its desecration by a foreign king and then arranged a festival procession into the Temple. There are many similarities between that occasion and Jesus' procession, even to the details of palm branches. So it appears likely that Jesus chose to copy the Maccabean procession. The parallel may be extended to include Matthew 21:12 in which he also cleanses the Temple. Jesus is making a point. He leads his attack against the corruption of the Sadduccees in the Temple rather than against the Romans. Jesus exposes their naked lust for power and their oppression of the common people, and in the process signs his own death warrant.

The description of Jesus' trial follows some very explicit teaching on the return of Jesus to judge the world. So one has the sense that Matthew is deliberately contrasting Jesus as the accused with Jesus the universal judge (Matthew 26:64). The pressure of the situation (a state of emergency) allows the Sanhedrin to suspend the normal

Velile Soha

rules of justice. The political fervour associated with Passover (the festival of liberation) together with Jesus' action against the Temple, leads the Sadducees to ally themselves with the Romans. It obviously did not take much persuasion to convince the Romans that Jesus was a threat to state security. The sentence is passed and Jesus is condemned to death by crucifixion.

Text
The theme of the kingship of Jesus emerges at several points in the narrative. One of the most dramatic pictures is found in Matthew 27:27-29, the mocking of Jesus. Condemned as a political agitator, Jesus is subjected to a most degrading process. Dressing him as a Roman (not Jewish) ruler, the soldiers of the guard pour abuse upon him, spitting and striking him again and again on his head with a wooden baton. Scarce wonder that Jesus is unable to carry his cross and that he dies so soon.

Crucifixion was reserved for rebellious slaves and revolutionaries. The victim was taken to the place of crucifixion in a procession, headed by a soldier bearing a plaque with the written accusation. Behind him came the victims each bearing the cross-piece upon which they were to hang. Once they reached the place of crucifixion, usually near a public road, they were tied or nailed to the cross-piece and then lifted up onto permanently embedded poles. Their feet were then nailed into the wooden pole: one foot on each side with nails through the ankles. (The person's feet were only just above ground — not high up as some paintings show.) To prolong the agony a small peglike seat was provided. Death by crucifixion could take up to five days. The victim was naked, and in order not to offend the Jewish men who might pass by, women were crucified facing towards the cross.

The Romans crucify Jesus and divide up his clothes among them (28:35). They keep watch (verse 36), presumably to prevent a rescue attempt. Verse 37 contains the charge, 'This is Jesus, the King of the Jews'. The Romans' sarcasm in describing Jesus as a king, rather than as a revolutionary or bandit, is used by Matthew to draw attention to the true kingship of Jesus. Verse 38 refers to the two 'robbers' on either side of Jesus. The Greek word used, *lestai*, means revolutionaries rather than thieves, which explains why such people were being crucified. So, Jesus is executed on a political charge together with two other political prisoners. A final touch is added when Matthew mentions that even these two people pour insults on Jesus (verse 44). The whole world has ganged up against the true King of Israel. What a picture of total rejection! The poor king has become the rejected king!

The reader, however, sees another side to the picture. Matthew uses the mocking of the crowd to draw attention to Jesus as both King and Son of God (verses 42ff). The reader is enabled to look beyond the mocking crowd and see what no human witness of the crucifixion could see. We, like Matthew's community, can draw encouragement from the scene, and so triumph over despair. Look at the contrast between verse 46 'My God, my God, why have you forsaken me?' and verse 51, 'At that moment the curtain of the Temple was torn in two from top to bottom.'

The first verse describes the utter desolation of Jesus who, as the representative child of humanity, takes upon himself the total suffering of all humankind. It sums up the feelings of those oppressed people who fear that even God has become a part of the oppressing system. 'Where are you God, now that I need you?'

The other verse describes one immediate result of Jesus' death, the tearing of the curtain (a double curtain) which separated the Holy of Holies from the rest of the Temple. This is the sign that God has now left the Temple. God's judgement has fallen upon the Temple! Rabbi Jonathan ben Zakkai, writing at the same time as Matthew, reports that forty years before its destruction in 70 AD, the doors of the Temple had come open of their own accord. He saw that as a sign of the coming destruction, and we should understand the torn curtain in the same way. Is it not curious that the two events both took place in 30 AD?

Matthew concludes the picture of Jesus' death with the cry of the centurion, 'Surely he was a (the) Son of God' (verse 54). So the death of the poor king, the judge of the world and the death of the only Son of God blend together.

For Matthew's community, the crucifixion represented Jesus' identification with them in their situation of rejection and persecution. They could reach out and take hold of that message and apply it to their own lives. Jesus' cry of desolation was on their own lips. At the same time they knew what it meant to have family snatched away from them, never to be seen again. So they had an insight into the heart of God during those dreadful hours at Golgotha.

Discussion

Together we shared our feelings and thoughts on the passage. One of the issues which came up was the terrible problem experienced here in South Africa of children in prison and parents hunting frantically to find them. In one case, the parents of a twelve year old girl spent more than six months searching for their daughter. We tried to think ourselves into the shoes of the parents, wondering how we would assure them of God's concern.

In your group you probably face a different set of situations. Perhaps the issues are different. Try to imagine how you would relate the death of Jesus to the people who suffer in your society. Some of our group were involved in the 'Free the Children' movement. What practical steps could you take to make the message of the crucified king real in your society?

JESUS AS PROPHET

The word 'prophet' conjures up different images in the minds of people. For many readers, a prophet would imply someone with psychic powers who can do strange and wonderful things, work miracles or predict the future. But what did the people of Jesus' time, like Matthew, understand by the title?

First and foremost the prophet was the messenger of God, bringing the word of God for a particular situation. The message was a combination of judgement and hope, and in some cases it was accompanied by symbolic actions. The Hebrew Bible is the pool out of which the people of Jesus' time drew their understanding of prophets, past or present. Matthew in turn dips into that pool for his/her powerful presentation of Jesus: teaching with the authority of Moses, healing with the power of Elijah, and speaking against the false prophets with the courage and conviction of Jeremiah.

The birth narratives, with Herod's pursuit of the infant Jesus, the killing of the babies in Bethlehem and the sojourn in Egypt are just a few of the parallels which Matthew draws between Jesus and Moses.

The most important parallel, however, is in the presentation of Jesus as the teacher and bearer of divine oracles. As Moses brought the Law to the people of Israel gathered at the foot of Mount Sinai, so Jesus reveals God's will for the Christian community of the new age. Moreover Jesus stands over and against the Scribes and Pharisees as the authentic interpreter of the Law of Moses. In other words, Jesus's teaching was not a denial of the Law of Moses, as some people believed, but rather is a continuation of that sacred tradition. God is once more choosing a community of people as a new covenantal partner and as the recipients of God's special relationship of love and mercy.

5. The Revelation of the Prophet

Matthew 5:38-42

Today's study is ideally suited for dramatization. So while one person read the Bible passage, two people played out the action of the three events, following the clues given in the exposition. The rest of our group were asked to watch the reactions of the players, and to jot down their observations. The two players had prepared well during the week and the reactions were superb. The aim of the exercise was to take note of the way in which the weaker person was able to seize the initiative from the stronger.

38 'You have heard that it was said, "Eye for eye, and tooth for tooth."
39 But I tell you, Do not resist an evil person. If someone strikes you on the right cheek, turn to him the other also.
40 And if someone wants to sue you and take your tunic, let him have your cloak as well.
41 If someone forces you to go one mile, go with him two miles.
42 Give to the one who asks you, and do not turn away from the one who wants to borrow from you.'

Matthew 5:38-42

After the drama we worked through the notes on the text.

Notes on the text

Background

Matthew's picture of Jesus as prophet began with Matthew 5, the Sermon on the Mount (see above p. 29). Here Matthew shows how Jesus resembles Moses, the first of the Hebrew prophets. We hear Jesus speaking with the same authority that once characterised Moses, the lawgiver. Jesus, however, does not bring a new law but shows his followers how to understand the old law in a new context. Jesus brings a sense of direction to people who have lost their way, a sense of hope for people who are living in the darkness of oppression, a sense of humanity for people who have forgotten what it means to be human.

After establishing in the opening set of blessings that the kingdom of God is good news for the poor, Matthew turns his attention to Jesus' instructions for righteous living. In verses 38-42 the particular concern is how to respond to evil and oppression.

Text

Jesus commences with the statement, 'an eye for an eye, a tooth for a tooth' (verse 38), which is a loose quotation of Exodus 21:24. The very same law was a point of debate between the different religious parties of Jesus' time, with some groups opting for a literal understanding of the law, and others advising a system of monetary compensation for the victim. In any event, it was a central pillar of Jewish civil legislation. If a person harmed you, you could harm them in the same way in return, or demand some compensation. Jesus takes issue with the literal interpretation of the law. Recognizing the dangers both of violent retribution and of the inherent cycle of violence, he offers a novel set of suggestions.

Jesus is not addressing the issue of revolution or war, but of personal response to acts of oppression. He gives people who are persecuted or exploited a way of responding which is non-violent but which at the same time allows the victim to seize the initiative against evil. Various situations are described and for each one Jesus advises a response.

Verse 39 speaks of being struck on the right cheek. Act out this process and you will find that Jesus implies a backhanded slap across the right cheek (presuming the opponent to be righthanded). Immediately we realise that the situation is that of a superior striking an inferior. In parts of South Africa this used to be called a 'kaffirklap'. We have a picture of the striker, large and offensive, and the victim, cringing and docile. The people of Jesus' time, and indeed of Matthew's time, knew the situation well. Indeed, Jewish law demanded higher compensation for the victim of such a blow than if one suffered a straight punch to the jaw. The backhanded slap was both a blow and an insult.

Well, what should one do? Jesus suggests that one should turn the head so as to present the left cheek, inviting another blow, but this time with a difference. The action would take the offender by surprise and force him/her to think about his/her next move. What is Jesus saying? It would appear that Jesus is offering the Christian a way of coping with a physical insult. When someone abuses you, turn your cheek - that is, take the initiative and force them to recognise you as a person. Do not let the offender rob you of your human dignity!

Verse 40 speaks of another situation familiar to the people of Palestine. The context here is a legal wrangle. A person wishes to sue you, presumably for an outstanding debt, and demands surety for its repayment. A wealthy person might give an item of jewellery or a valuable object, but a poor person probably had only the clothes which he or she wore. In this case the person has taken the clothes of the victim but has left their cloak. This is most unusual, for the cloak was the normal pledge. However under Jewish law (Exodus 22:26ff), the cloak of a person could not be retained overnight, for the cloak was both coat and bedclothes for the person and their family. On a bitterly cold winter's evening the loss of the mother's/father's cloak would be a particularly serious threat to the well-being of the younger children. However, by taking the clothes of the victim, there was no legal obligation to return the pledge at nightfall.

Jesus is once again addressing a situation of injustice. Someone has taken your clothes and clearly does not intend to return them until the debt is paid. Now, a set of clothes could take many months to replace, for the average wage only covered the food needed by the family. Once again, Jesus presumes a state of oppression where the poor have no recourse to the law. Both the stolen clothes and the backhand slap are crimes against the weak and defenceless. What should one do? Fight back? No, Jesus offers a better way. Give them the legal pledge of your cloak as well, then to their horror and amazement, walk away naked. The shock and humour that this action would generate would have an unforgettable effect on the watchers. Certainly it would represent a victory for the otherwise defenceless person.

So, Jesus offers us a way of responding to injustice which is funny, challenging and above all designed to secure both the initiative in the drama and the retention of human dignity.

Verse 41 addresses a military question. As an occupied territory, the people of Judaea were obliged to render manual labour for the Roman soldiers. A person was legally required to carry the baggage of a soldier for no more than one thousand paces. Thereafter the soldier would have to find another porter. In such a case, Jesus suggests another way of seizing the initiative. 'Walk two thousand paces', he says. Imagine the surprise of the Roman soldier, who after stopping to rest at a tavern or under some trees, sets out to find his baggage — now two thousand paces down the road. Perhaps he would incur the wrath of a senior officer, perhaps the humour of the locals. At the very least, he would hesitate to co-opt your services in the future.

In the verses that follow (verses 42-48) Jesus speaks about the process of giving. This is an essential part of the Christian response to evil. The way of the world is the way of returning evil for evil. The way of Jesus is returning good for evil, love for hate. Take the initiative by non-violent means and in all things retain your human dignity and allow others to do the same. 'You can't take away my dignity' says the song, but it is wrong. Everyday people are being stripped of their dignity by the fingers of structural violence. Jesus recognises the need to hold on to one's dignity at all costs.

Discussion

We spent time suggesting some contemporary problems which people face, and different ways of responding to them. We recalled some ways in which Christians had coped with the State of Emergency in South Africa. Having the police interrogator around for dinner was one Christian's response to a period of detention without trial. What could have been a source of bitter resentment became instead a victory for Christian love. You might have read or heard of similar stories which you could relate to the group. Think of your own situation and the way in which Christians could help people to cope with injustices and oppression.

The object of this exercise was to help people to measure their response by the standards set in the Sermon on the Mount. We came to realise that such behaviour required a complete re-ordering of our day-to-day lives. The group leader was careful to point out that non-violence was not a betrayal of the cause for liberation nor a sign of weakness. Jesus was not asking Christians to be doormats to be stamped upon, but rather to use the greater force — that of forgiving love. Then in conclusion we read the reflection, and used it as a lead-in to a time of prayer.

Reflection

The line of men moved steadily forward like a grotesque caterpillar. There was no pushing or shoving, just a gentle movement towards the gates where the men in uniform stood. The dull thud of the weapons of the guards was the macabre music to which the caterpillar danced. Slowly like a dream the duel played itself out, the clothes of the men turned from white to red, but still they walked the never ending circle. As they fell, willing hands lifted them up, wiped the blood and helped them find their weary way to the back of the line. On and on, until their eyes no longer focussed and the guards were wearied with their own terrible battering against this mass of human suffering. Gandhi understood what few people learn, that violence is always the last resort - a sign of weakness, not of strength.

6. The Task of the Prophet

Matthew 10:34-42

We started the session with a short discussion on contemporary prophets. After naming people like Desmond Tutu, Alan Boesak, and Beyers Naude (you may wish to include people from your own society), we tried to decide what qualities a modern prophet displayed. We soon became aware of an interesting detail. The prophet and his/her message are tightly bound together. For a believable message, there had to be a livable expression. Unless the prophet lived out the message in their own lives, no one else could be expected to take that message seriously.

We read the Biblical passage and, in turn, commented on one thing which we personally found to be 'thought provoking'.

³⁴ 'Do not suppose that I have come to bring peace to the earth. I did not come to bring peace, but a sword.

³⁵ For I have come to turn

"a man against his father,
a daughter against her mother,
a daughter-in-law against her mother-in-law —
³⁶ a man's enemies will be the members of his own household."

³⁷ Anyone who loves his father or mother more than me is not worthy of me; anyone who loves his son or daughter more than me is not worthy of me;

³⁸ and anyone who does not take his cross and follow me is not worthy of me.

³⁹ Whoever finds his life will lose it, and whoever loses his life for my sake will find it.

⁴⁰ He who receives you receives me, and he who receives me receives the one who sent me.

⁴¹ Anyone who receives a prophet because he is a prophet will receive a prophet's reward, and anyone who receives a righteous man because he is a righteous man will receive a righteous man's reward.

⁴² And if anyone gives a cup of cold water to one of these little ones because he is my disciple, I tell you the truth, he will certainly not lose his reward.'

Matthew 10:34-42

After this the group considered how Jesus' words often provoked divisions among the people eg John 7:40-43 and 9:16. We saw how some people followed him , but others rejected everything he stood for. We thought about whether the words of Jesus still provoke division. We came to realise that speaking the truth could often cause division. You may think of some examples from your own experience. We spent a short time debating whether it was preferable to keep silent rather than to cause division. Obviously it depended on the situation. Then we turned to the notes.

Notes on the text

Background

The Sermon on the Mount comes to an end at Matthew 8:1 and there follows a series of healings and miracles (chapters 8 and 9). In chapter 10, Jesus calls together the twelve disciples and sends them out into the region of Judaea. They are to be as wise as serpents and as innocent as doves (10:16). Jesus then warns of the coming age of persecutions, both Jewish (verse 17) and Roman (verse 18) in origin. Here Matthew is speaking directly to the community in Antioch and assuring them not only of the dangers about them, but also of God's gracious protection (verses 26-31). At this point there is a distinct change of tone.

Jesus now addresses the question of his mission. Like the prophets of old he comes to bring the message of God, a message of judgement and hope. In this case, it is a hard message for his listeners to hear, but it ends with a promise.

Text

Verse 34 commences with an astonishing claim. 'Do not suppose that I have come to bring peace to the earth. I did not come to bring peace, but a sword.' Is this not in direct contradiction to the teaching we have just studied from the Sermon on the Mount? Surely there is an advocate here for violent revolution. Certainly some people have tried to use this text to justify Christians using force to overthrow unjust regimes. But that is not what Jesus is trying to say. Here, as in the Sermon on the Mount, Jesus is not concerned with laying down rules for or against armed resistance. What he is describing is the consequences of the Christian message and its impact upon the life of a person. It is a divisive message. By its inherent nature, it creates conflict. This is because the Christian message of justice and freedom is inimical to anything evil or base.

The word 'sword' in Matthew's version of this saying of Jesus' is rendered as *schisma* or division by Luke (Luke 12:51-53). Both Matthew and Luke used a common source called 'Q', which, as we have seen, was a collection of important sayings of Jesus. Sometimes Matthew and Luke paraphrase the words of Jesus found in Q and at other times they report them verbatim. When one has to choose between two readings or as here two words, the usual rule is to adopt the more difficult reading as the original and to see the other as a paraphrase.

The people of Jesus' time used very graphic language, and the allegories and expressions are often shocking to our ears.

In choosing the word 'sword' as the more difficult reading we would hold to Matthew's version as being Jesus' original words, and Luke's version as rendering the sense of those words. Jesus is therefore the one who, like a surgeon, cuts away the flesh to reveal the cancerous growth. Jesus comes to destroy evil, but first he has to expose it, hence the division — the cutting of the sword. The Church too has a part to play in this process of defeating evil, and that was true for Matthew's church as well as our own.

Verses 35ff continues the account of the division. One person will be set against another — even within families. The reason for this extraordinary statement is apparent when we consider the likely consequences of a member of a family becoming a Christian. For example, a family might be Gentile (non-Jewish) in origin and committed to traditional Roman or Egyptian deities. Suddenly one member of the family becomes a Christian and their values change. In a real way Jesus has set this person against their family, and from that point on there will be conflict, tension and pressure as the family attempts to bring the person back into line. This was a reality for Matthew's church in Antioch where the mainly third generation Christians were far enough removed from their Jewish roots to know at first hand the effects of families divided by Christianity. Today the same is true when, for example, a Jew or Muslim becomes a Christian.

We can imagine the subtle ways in which a family could try and break down the resolve of a young Christian. Perhaps there would even be an ultimatum — Jesus or us! What courage it would take to hold on to one's beliefs in that situation. So Jesus warns of the pressures both overt and subtle which families and society will bring to bear upon the Christian.

In verse 37 it is Matthew's turn to render the sense of Jesus' words rather than repeating their closest Greek equivalent, found in Luke 12:51-53 (he or she who does not *hate* their father...). Again this hyperbolic language (exaggeration for effect) warns us to look beyond the literal sense of the words. We may be assured that Jesus does not want us to hate our parents. Rather, as Matthew puts it, we are to prefer allegiance to Jesus above all other claims. This does not mean abandoning or neglecting our family.

Verse 38 speaks of taking up one's cross. Matthew and his readers would of course be familiar with Jesus' death by crucifixion. Here the reference is to carrying a load in a general sense but with the added nuance that it is a back-breaking one. The load may be living in a non-Christian family, or suffering oppression. We are called upon to carry these burdens and not to crumble beneath them. The cross kills, but it can still be carried. This is more than submission, this is the spirit of resistance. It is a call to a new style of living.

So, Jesus the prophet describes his task on earth: to call people to a new life style (verse 39) and to commission others to take his place (verse 40). His disciples are in turn to be prophets, going out in the name of the prophet Jesus (verse 41). And they will receive the same reward, for they too will be raised in the last days. But there is an implicit note of warning: the path of a prophet is the path of suffering. Matthew's community well knew this truth.

Finally, Jesus promises that all those who show kindness to the suffering Christians (literally little ones or humble folk), will also be rewarded (verse 42). Remember the parable of the king dividing the sheep and goats!

Discussion

We returned to our discussion of the situations in which Jesus' words provoked division and the way in which people, and even families, can become divided. Some divisions are caused by true teaching but others by lies. So a society might be divided by racism or sexism but this was clearly not the kind of division which Jesus brought. We then considered the reflection, which dealt with the situation in Crossroads, Cape Town. In 1986, according to one account, a group of older men were bribed by the police to burn down the shacks of the younger 'comrades'. These older men had been promised better housing once the other group had been chased away. Here was a clear example of how greed can divide a society. Perhaps you can think of a more topical example for your own use. Our prime objective was to distinguish the teaching of Jesus, which highlights good and exposes evil, from ideologies like apartheid, which create false divisions among people.

Reflection

The flames of the burning shacks mounted to the skies like the wings of a primaeval bird from some ancient legend. The cries of sorrow, pain and trapped-burning death clamoured at the ears of the old men standing silently by. Their hands still held the flaming torches, their eyes still glazed with senseless anger and their pockets jingled with their 'Judas' fee.

Between these old men and their young enemies stood no barrier of race, or tribe, or social standing. Some of them could remember carrying these boys as children, playing with them in the fields, and teaching them to be men. Now flaming fingers separated them from each other, tore apart the heart of the family and drove oppressed against oppressed, like trapped animals fighting each other to be free.

Falsehood like truth divides, but only for selfish motives.

We closed in prayer, trying to focus on what God is saying to our society, and how we can be his prophets. Is God saying something to you? To your society? What will your response be?

7. True and False Teachers

Matthew 23:1-13, 23, 25, 27-31

We began the session by summarizing what we had discovered about Matthew's picture of Jesus as a prophet. Using a copy of the picture of Jesus (see page 31), the leader had made a poster, with the picture in the very centre. We were asked to respond to Matthew's presentation of Jesus as prophet by writing a word or phrase on pre-cut pieces of card. Then, each in turn, we were given the opportunity to place our card on the poster and to say why we had chosen that description. Words like 'truth', 'division' and 'authority' appeared.

Using this reflection, the leader lead us into a discussion on true and false teaching, in society and also in the Church. What is the situation in your country? Use the reflection to think about what happens in your society.

Reflection

You meet them everywhere, crying at the corners of the city streets, speaking smooth-sounding words over television channels, addressing military parades with stirring words against painted dragons in the sky. With glib smiling faces, they utter the same myths over and again until weary minds no longer know what to believe. THEY ARE THE PROPHETS OF THE STATE, the prophets of untruth, of injustice and oppression. Desperately twisting reality for their own ends, they plunder the minds of the people. With their weapons of selective censorship, they create an illusory world. Propped up between the pillars of military control and economic exploitation, they fear nothing but truth. But their songs of victory are really dirges, as, blinded by their own lies, they fail to see that they are dancing along the very edge of a bottomless chasm.

After a short discussion, we read the set passage and worked through the notes.

Jesus said to the crowds and to his disciples:

2 'The teachers of the law and the Pharisees sit in Moses' seat.

3 So you must obey them and do everything they tell you. But do not do what they do, for they do not practise what they preach.

4 They tie up heavy loads and put them on men's shoulders, but they themselves are not willing to lift a finger to move them.

5 Everything they do is done for men to see: They make their phylacteries wide and the tassels of their prayer shawls long;

6 they love the place of honour at banquets and the most important seats in the synagogues;

7 they love to be greeted in the marketplaces and to have men call them "Rabbi".

8 'But you are not to be called "Rabbi", for you have only one Master and you are all brothers.

9 And do not call anyone on earth "father", for you have one Father, and he is in heaven.

10 Nor are you to be called "teacher", for you have one Teacher, the Christ.

11 The greatest among you will be your servant.

12 For whoever exalts himself will be humbled, and whoever humbles himself will be exalted.

13 Woe to you, teachers of the law and Pharisees, you hypocrites! You shut the kingdom of heaven in men's faces. You yourselves do not enter, nor will you let those enter who are trying to.

23 Woe to you, teachers of the law and Pharisees, you hypocrites! You give a tenth of your spices — mint, dill and cummin. But you have neglected the more important matters of the law — justice, mercy and faithfulness. You should have practised the latter, without neglecting the former.

25 Woe to you, teachers of the law and Pharisees, you hypocrites! You clean the outside of the cup and dish, but inside they are full of greed and self-indulgence.

27 Woe to you, teachers of the law and Pharisees, you hypocrites! You are like whitewashed tombs, which look beautiful on the outside but on the inside are full of dead men's bones and everything unclean.

28 In the same way, on the outside you appear to people as righteous but on the inside you are full of hypocrisy and wickedness.

29 Woe to you, teachers of the law and Pharisees, you hypocrites! You build tombs for the prophets and decorate the graves of the righteous.

30 And you say, "If we had lived in the days of our forefathers, we would not have taken part with them in shedding the blood of the prophets."

31 So you testify against yourselves that you are the descendants of those who murdered the prophets.'

Matthew 23:1-13, 23, 25, 27-31

Notes on the text

Background

Jeremiah is the prophet of the Hebrew Bible who is renowned for his scathing attack upon the false prophets. Ignoring reality, these prophets assured the people of their political safety. Holding on to a twisted understanding of the words of Isaiah of Jerusalem, they attempted to lead the people into believing that God would not punish them for their sins. Like blind guides, they tottered at the edge of a precipice, all the while mouthing words of reassurance to the people about them.

Jesus, like Jeremiah, exposes the false teaching of his day. Here, in Matthew 23, we have a collection of seven terrible accusations spoken by Jesus. The targets of his attack were the teachers of the Law — the scribes and the Pharisees. The scribes were the academics of Israel, the equivalent of university professors, concerned with the detailed study of the Jewish Law. The Pharisees were the ordinary religious teachers, mainly concerned with the instruction of the local people in the synagogues. What had these people done to warrant the scathing attack of Jesus? We can understand Jesus' critique of the wealthy Sadducees who exploited the poor of Judaea, but what had the scribes and Pharisees done that was so terrible? As we read the woes recorded in Matthew 23, an answer emerges.

Text

Jesus commences his critique with a reminder of the calling of all Jewish teachers. They are to 'sit in Moses's seat' (verse 2). In other words, they had inherited the responsibilty once held by Moses. But there the similarity with Moses ends. Their lives were in complete contradiction to the words they utter. As verse 3 puts it, 'they do not practice what they preach'.

Jesus deplores the outward show of these religious leaders (verses 5-7), and insists that his followers should be different. Prophet-like, he calls them to be part of an alternative society (verses 8-12). Turning upside down contemporary values and norms, Jesus urges Christians to be servants of their Servant Lord. The traditional titles of honour, master, teacher or lord have no place in a Christian society. Jesus calls for an egalitarian society (a society of equals) and this challenge is perhaps one of his most revolutionary statements.

In a devastating attack, Jesus strips away the outward pretence of holiness and exposes the hypocrisy of the religious teachers. Seven times he utters the word 'woe', like a deep groan of anguish. With each cry he opens up another aspect of the shallowness of their teaching. For example, they rule over who may or may not enter the kingdom of God (verse 13), blocking the path of the poor and depriving them of their rightful education. In the opinion of these men, the poor were unworthy of education and were therefore excluded from the knowledge of God.

Perhaps the most telling line of Jesus, is where he describes the concern of the scribes and Pharisees with tithing (verse 23). While they worry about petty issues like tithing one's herb garden, the weightier matters of justice, mercy and faithfulness are forgotten. So their religion is a sham in the sight of God, a front for their manipulation of the people for their own evil purposes. Like the whitewashed graves of Silwan, opposite Jerusalem, they look beautiful on the outside, but inside lurks the death of greed and self-indulgence (verses 25-28). Pretending to be the friends of the common people, they are in fact their oppressors.

Jesus discerns their hatred of the truth of God, as they secretly clamour for the blood of the prophets (verses 29-32). They and their kind are the enemies of truth, the masters of propaganda. Putting themselves up as the sole discerners of the will of God, they try to discredit all who oppose them. So the Tutu's of this world are branded as communists and heretics. And people like their saviour, Jesus, will be put to death, condemned as teachers of lies and political agitators.

Discussion

In a brief discussion we contrasted Jesus' teaching with that of the scribe's and Pharisees. We came to realize that these men were chosen by Jesus for rebuff because of their honourable position. They, like the prophets of old, were the people entrusted by God with the task of conveying his message to the people, but they had failed.

We spent some time thinking about our responsibility, as Christians, in the face of false teaching. Finally we closed in prayer, with a particular focus on living lives that mirrored our beliefs and the truth of the Christian message.

You may wish to pick up some particular issue in your own community which relates to this teaching of Jesus. Are there modern counterparts to the scribes and Pharisees? What do they teach? What are some of the possible Christian responses to such people?

8. The Prophetic Hope

Matthew 24:1-21, 23-25, 27, 31

For the last of the studies on Jesus, the Prophet, we began by reading the reflection and then in turn sharing a brief picture of our hope for the future.

Reflection

Raindrops pattered on the green plastic tent, growing in intensity or fading according to the force of the wind. Inside, carefully positioned to avoid the puddles, sat a mother, surrounded by her meagre possessions. Her child was sleeping. Gently she kissed the dirty forehead. Soft-eyed she lost herself in the joy of her child, until the gnawing pangs of hunger awoke her to the present. Without work there was no money, without money there was no food. Who would have thought that life could be reduced to such a simple equation?

A fresh gust of wind shook the shanty-tent and for a moment seemed ready to strip it to pieces. Then it passed and the woman breathed again. Her thoughts turned to ponder her situation anew and to experience once more the cruelty of it all. She was beyond hatred now. There had been a time for that, when her first child had died in the muddy streets. Well she remembered that time, with the waves of violent anger, the clenched fists and the choking tears. Now all that had passed, leaving her stripped of emotion, seemingly beyond caring. On the brink of despair she hesitated as, through a tear in the plastic, she saw the rainbow. Like a child's smile it re-kindled the flame of hope within her. If not in her own lifetime, then in the lifetime of her child. Softly her lips formed a song of her youth. God would remember her people. The guardian spirits of Africa, of South America, and of Palestine stood in God's presence. God would hear one day, soon.

After we had shared our hopes for the future, we spoke about the Christian hope for the return of Jesus and the arrival of the kingdom. We read together from Isaiah 9:2-7, and then tried to imagine what the people of Jesus' own time might have hoped for. After a short discussion, we worked through the notes together.

Jesus left the temple and was walking away when his disciples came up to him to call his attention to its buildings.

2 'Do you see all these things?' he asked. 'I tell you the truth, not one stone here will be left on another; every one will be thrown down.'

3 As Jesus was sitting on the Mount of Olives, the disciples came to him privately. 'Tell us', they said, 'when will this happen, and what will be the sign of your coming and of the end of the age?'

4 Jesus answered: 'Watch out that no one deceives you.

5 For many will come in my name, claiming, "I am the Christ," and will deceive many.

6 You will hear of wars and rumours of wars, but see to it that you are not alarmed. Such things must happen, but the end is still to come.

7 Nation will rise against nation, and kingdom against kingdom. There will be famines and earthquakes in various places.

8 All these are the beginning of birth pains.

9 Then you will be handed over to be persecuted and put to death, and you will be hated by all nations because of me.

¹⁰ At that time many will turn away from the faith and will betray and hate each other,

¹¹ and many false prophets will appear and deceive many people.

¹² Because of the increase of wickedness, the love of most will grow cold,

¹³ but he who stands firm to the end will be saved.

¹⁴ And this gospel of the kingdom will be preached in the whole world as a testimony to all nations, and then the end will come.

¹⁵ So when you see standing in the holy place "the abomination that causes desolation", spoken of through the prophet Daniel — let the reader understand —

¹⁶ then let those who are in Judea flee to the mountains.

¹⁷ Let no one on the roof of his house go down to take anything out of the house.

¹⁸ Let no one in the field go back to get his cloak.

¹⁹ How dreadful it will be in those days for pregnant women and nursing mothers!

²⁰ Pray that your flight will not take place in winter or on the Sabbath.

²¹ For then there will be great distress, unequalled from the beginning of the world until now — and never to be equalled again.

²³ At that time if anyone says to you, "Look, here is the Christ!" or, "There he is!" do not believe it.

²⁴ For false Christs and false prophets will appear and perform great signs and miracles to deceive even the elect — if that were possible.

²⁵ See, I have told you ahead of time.

²⁷ For as the lightning comes from the east and flashes to the west, so will be the coming of the Son of Man.

³¹ And he will send his angels with a loud trumpet call, and they will gather his elect from the four winds, from one end of the heavens to the other.'

Matthew 24:1-21, 23-25, 27, 31

Notes on the text

Background

The people of Jesus' time looked forward to the coming of God's kingdom. Two main ideas were to be found. Some people expected a historical kingdom like David's. Daily they prayed that the Romans would be overthrown and a kingdom of justice would prevail (*cf* Isaiah 9:1-3). One of the Jewish prayers of the time contains the line, 'May the arrogant kingdom be rooted out in our days' and the plea

'Look upon our affliction (oppression) and plead our cause, and redeem us speedily for thy name's sake; for thou art a mighty redeemer.'

Other people, influenced by writings like Daniel 7, looked for the coming of a supernatural kingdom which would suddenly break into this world. This kingdom would be completely different from any earthly experience. For people who had had their hopes for the reform of the present world smashed time and again, such an other-worldly hope was able to transcend their bitter plight.

Jesus' teaching blends Isaiah's hope for a kingdom of justice and righteousness with the supernatural elements of Daniel. So Jesus promises that God's kingdom will truly come on earth, but that it will not be just an ordinary kingdom. God's kingdom will be a universal kingdom instituted by God through Jesus. The kingdom will come with the return of Jesus. This was a major issue for Matthew's community, living forty years after the resurrection of Jesus. In fact the whole of Matthew 24 is devoted to this teaching, so we can sense both the expectation and the disillusionment which the people of that community felt.

Text
Jesus begins with a prophecy concerning Jerusalem. The disciples are overcome with admiration for the grandness of Herod's huge Temple. In contrast, Jesus speaks of its coming destruction (verse 2). Like Jeremiah of old, Jesus foretells the pouring out of God's wrath on the city. In 70 AD, when the Roman army descended upon the foothills of Judaea, the prophecy came true.

The speedy fulfilment of this prophecy led the Christians of Matthew's time to expect the imminent arrival of the kingdom of God in all its fulness, and so they carefully treasured all Jesus' other promises — especially as Roman persecution increased. However, some had begun to realise that the end might not come as quickly as everyone hoped it would and it is for these people, grown weary of waiting and perhaps led astray by other messiahs, that Matthew includes Jesus' words on the 'delayed' time (verses 3-14). Yes, one will feel surely that this must be the time of the end. As oppression (tribulation) increases, as people cry out to God from the depths of their suffering, false prophets will arise preaching a gospel of lies (verse 11). Verse 14 announces that the good news of Jesus will be heard in all the world and then the end shall come. This is not a timetable for calculating the return of Jesus; rather it is Jesus' way of saying that the kingdom of God is for all nations, not just for the Jews.

The remainder of the chapter touches again on Jesus' teaching about the destruction of Jerusalem (verses 15-21) and the delay in Jesus' return (verses 23-26). Clearly many in Matthew's community believed that they were living in the last days, and apparently they were plagued by false prophets (verse 24). In the midst of all the confusion Matthew uses Jesus' words to call the Church back to its true task — confessing Jesus (verse 9). Do not be like those who fall away, betray one another to the authorities, and show hate (verse 10): in a world where it is so easy for the oppressed to turn on one another, these words speak with great authority.

Finally Matthew points the church to the hope of Jesus' return as prophesied by the Son of Man in Daniel 7:13 (verse 27). This mysterious figure, clearly superhuman, had long baffled the minds of Jesus' contemporaries. Now the mystery is revealed. Jesus will come as the triumphant Son of Man (Child of Humanity) with the armies of heaven to defeat the powers of evil and oppression once and for all (verses 31, 51). Truly this is a message of hope for all people who know what it is to be without hope.

So we witness the power of Matthew's portrait of Jesus as prophet. We feel the authority of Jesus as the proclaimer of God's judgement, and his wonderful message of hope for the hopeless. What a Saviour!

Discussion

We shared in a brief discussion on the tension experienced by Christians between our hope for the future and the present reality. As Christians we believe that evil will only be vanquished completely when Jesus returns, but all through history God has demonstrated the ongoing war with evil. Christians are also a part of this process, working here and now for a new world and a society ruled by justice and integrity. The liberation of the oppressed is both a part of God's plan for the present, as well as a part of the future, when Jesus comes as king.

We concluded by praying for a greater hope for our land and for its future. We prayed that as Christians we would, like Matthew's church, learn to trust in the promises of God, and to expect the vanquishing of evil in our own time. After the prayer time we felt a need to speak about our commitment to doing something about the future. Perhaps your group will feel the same. These were some of our suggestions.

1. To identify with those who are oppressed, by caring for the families of detainees and attending funerals of 'unrest victims' (people killed in the conflict between police/army and the people of black townships).

2. To join an existing political or welfare organization, rather than attempting to set up parallel organizations.

3. To find ways to fight the apathy of so many people, who sit back while the most terrible events take place within a few kilometres of their homes.

4. To write letters to the press or to members of parliament.

JESUS AS SON OF GOD

All the other titles which Matthew attributes to Jesus pale into insignificance when compared with the title Son of God. Here is an expression of majesty greater than that of king, a description of authority beyond that of prophet. Jesus is the Son of God, and that is what makes him different from all other agents of God.

What is the central message of Matthew's Gospel? For a group of frightened Christian believers at the end of the first century, the message is that of the presence of God in the community of the Church. Remember that the Gospel starts with the title Immanuel (God with us) and ends with the promise of Jesus' ongoing presence. The title Son of God explains the connection between the human Jesus and the divinity of God. Here lies Matthew's leap of faith. Like so many Christians of the first century, Matthew realised that in an amazing way the ongoing presence of the resurrected Jesus was at the same time the presence of God.

What does the title Son of God mean? As the Son of God Jesus is the unique representative of God. Indeed he shares the attributes of God and so is worthy of being worshipped and adored. Matthew clearly understood what centuries of scholars would subsequently struggle to describe, namely that in some mystical way Jesus and God were one. How does Matthew show this truth? As we read the Gospel we see that the disciples worship Jesus. We find that God himself reveals to Peter that Jesus is his Son, and we hear Jesus telling his disciples that only he knows the heart and will of God, his Father. These are some of the passages which will form the focus of the third and last section of our studies.

9. The Miracles of the Son

Matthew 14:22-33

We spent some time talking about family likenesses. We compared stories about ways in which we take after one or both of our parents. Then we moved on to meditate on Matthew 11:27 and the sense of closeness expressed there between Jesus and God.

> 'All things have been committed to me by my Father. No one knows the Son except the Father, and no one knows the Father except the Son and those to whom the Son chooses to reveal him.'
>
> *Matthew 11:27*

Finally we turned our attention to the Bible passage. Instead of one person reading the section, we chose to read it as if it were a drama. Two people took the parts of Jesus and Peter respectively, while a narrator filled in the rest of the story. The rest of the group were the disciples, making appropriate comments and noises.

22 Jesus made the disciples get into the boat and go on ahead of him to the other side, while he dismissed the crowd.

23 After he had dismissed them, he went up into the hills by himself to pray. When evening came, he was there alone,

24 but the boat was already a considerable distance from land, buffeted by the waves because the wind was against it.

25 During the fourth watch of the night Jesus went out to them, walking on the lake.

26 When the disciples saw him walking on the lake, they were terrified. 'It's a ghost', they said, and cried out in fear.

27 But Jesus immediately said to them: 'Take courage! It is I. Don't be afraid.'

28 'Lord, if it's you', Peter replied, 'tell me to come to you on the water.'

29 'Come', he said. Then Peter got down out of the boat and walked on the water to Jesus.

30 But when he saw the wind, he was afraid and, beginning to sink, cried out, 'Lord, save me!'

31 Immediately Jesus reached out his hand and caught him. 'You of little faith', he said, 'why did you doubt?'

32 And when they climbed into the boat, the wind died down.

33 Then those who were in the boat worshipped him, saying, 'Truly you are the Son of God.'

Matthew 14:22-33

We were asked what we thought was distinctive about Matthew's account of the story, when compared with the other three Gospels. (See Mark 6:45-52, Luke 8:22-25, John 6:16-21.) After various suggestions were made we read the notes together.

Notes on the text

Background

The meaning of Jesus' miracles may be found in his teaching. He was therefore not just a worker of miracles like Hanina ben Dosa or Honi the circle-drawer, who lived in Israel shortly after the time of Jesus. Honi drew a circle in the dust and prayed for rain. He refused to leave the circle until God answered his prayer, and God did indeed send the rain. Hanina was a Jewish peasant living in Galilee whose prayers brought about several wonderful acts of God, including the healing of Rabbi Gamaliel's son. Without leaving his humble dwelling, Hanina told the messengers from Gamaliel that the son would be cured and, indeed, he was cured that very hour.

Such parallels with the miracles of Jesus are striking. What then is different about Jesus' miracles you may ask? When the miracles and teaching of Jesus are linked we understand that the miracles are signs of the coming of God's kingdom. In God's kingdom there will be no more sickness, oppression or death. So the miracles of Jesus anticipate the day when the kingdom will be here on earth in all its fullness. A new exodus has begun.

The feeding of the people in the wilderness (Matthew 14:14-21) was a reminder of Moses' work and the manna which fell from heaven (*cf*

John 6). Jewish tradition promised that the coming king would perform the same miracles as those performed by Moses. The feeding miracle is therefore a confirmation of that promise. But the miracle which follows, when Jesus walks on the water, is something new, although it vaguely resembles Moses' crossing of the Red Sea. Matthew will use this new miracle to set Jesus apart from all previous agents of God, even Moses.

Text

With the feeding completed, Jesus instructs the disciples to sail across the lake (verse 22). This allows Jesus (verse 23) to spend time alone on the hilltop in prayer. The crossing, however, turns into a nightmare as the wind whips the lake into a violent storm. Just before dawn Jesus appears to the disciples. 'Horrors, this is a ghost!' they cry. At this time it was thought that the dead were confined to a place called Sheol. Occasionally, however, one might escape from this underworldly prison to roam the earth as a 'shade' or shadowy representative of his or her former self.

Jesus reassures the disciples (verse 27) and Peter is encouraged to step out of the boat (verse 28ff). Peter, of course, was a popular figure in Matthew's community, following his great missionary work in Antioch. The story of Peter's unequal struggle with the waves (verse 30) had a yet deeper meaning for Matthew's community. They too were surrounded by waves, the waves of Jewish persecution and Roman savagery. So they could share both Peter's fears and his joy when Jesus stretches out a helping hand. And let us not forget the message in that little Greek word *euthos* in verse 31 meaning 'immediately'. In moments of great danger, Jesus acts immediately.

The challenge of Jesus to Peter 'You of little faith, why did you doubt?' is also a message for Matthew's community. In the midst of the rising wave of persecution, some people are deserting their faith (Matthew 23:10). Doubts are rampant (Matthew 28:17). Bravely,

Matthew's Jesus calls to the community to hold fast, to take hold of his hand and to leave their doubts behind.

The wind stops without another word from Jesus (verse 32), and here we find the answer to the question posed earlier. The disciples turn in adoration to Jesus and worship him as the Son of God. None of the other Gospels record this incident. Matthew, therefore, has singled

Velile Soha

out the calming of the sea as a platform from which to announce the divinity of Jesus. The response of the disciples in worshipping Jesus and confessing him as Son of God indicates the right response to Jesus' display of authority. This is no ordinary messiah or common prophet. This Jesus is the chosen Son of God, who alone with the Father/Mother God is worthy to be praised.

The note of assurance remains with Matthew's community and with us. God sees us in our moment of need and comes to set us free. The Son of God is Immanuel, God with us. This is the message which triumphs over persecution, oppression and violence. For 'Surely the arm of the Lord is not too short to save, nor is his ear too dull to hear' (Isaiah 59:1).

Discussion

We spent some time relating the picture of assurance to our contemporary situation. We were asked what assurance we could bring as Christians to the following people (you may wish to add to the list):

a A widow living in poverty
b A young person alienated from their family
c A person imprisoned on false charges.

Some of the group felt that the assurance of God's concern was not enough. They felt that some tangible action on the part of the Christian assurer was necessary. Like Jesus, we needed to be stretching out our hands in some practical way. We were then encouraged to describe some possible areas where we could, as a group, become involved in bringing such assurance.

We closed with the reflection.

Reflection

Locked in a silent world of concrete and bars, sentenced to darkness and the stench of open latrines, touched only by the calloused fists of angry wardens, condemned for caring too much. For attending a funeral of a friend, for reaching out to protect a fellow mourner from a policeman's quirt (whip) and for encouraging little school children not to be afraid. There was no trial, no questioning after the first few days, only the complete aloneness and the waves of depression that broke across her back, like a calculated scourging. Angry with herself for the fears and the tears, but unable to find any other escape from the maze of her tormented mind. Desperately she longed for the assurance that, somehow, somebody understood her pain and shared just a little of it. And how we longed that we could reach you, to encourage you and to build up that flame within your heart before it died and you sank beneath the waves.

10. The Parables of the Son

Matthew 21:33-46

The previous sessions had been rather serious, so the group decided to change the tone for this study. We were each asked to describe a childhood memory, preferably something funny. At the end of half an hour we felt that we knew each other a little better. The nature of the previous studies had placed a strain on all of us, so that it was good to be able to laugh together. We were amazed at how different our experiences of childhood had been.

We commented upon a few of the more obvious differences and then spoke about privilege and responsibility. We thought back to the rich of Jesus' time, particularly the Sadducees and Pharisees. They had the advantage of wealth and education, particularly religious education. But they did not take up the consequent responsibilities. So the message of God's care and concern was blocked. The people who so desperately needed to hear it never did. They were called the *Am ha Aretz* or 'the people of the land' and, condemned as illiterate, treated as second class citizens, no better than the heathen, they were deemed unworthy of God's concern.

We were encouraged to relate the situation to our own context. Who were the 'people of the land ' in our society? Who are they in your society? After some discussion, we were reminded briefly of Jesus' verbal attack on the privileged who ignored their responsibilities (Matthew 23), then we read the study passage silently and shared the notes.

33 'Listen to another parable: There was a landowner who planted a vineyard. He put a wall around it, dug a winepress in it and built a watchtower. Then he rented the vineyard to some farmers and went away on a journey.

34 When the harvest time approached, he sent his servants to the tenants to collect his fruit.

35 The tenants seized his servants; they beat one, killed another, and stoned a third.

36 Then he sent other servants to them, more than the first time, and the tenants treated them the same way.

37 Last of all, he sent his son to them. "They will respect my son," he said.

38 But when the tenants saw the son, they said to each other. "This is the heir. Come, let's kill him and take his inheritance."

39 So they took him and threw him out of the vineyard and killed him.

40 Therefore, when the owner of the vineyard comes, what will he do to those tenants?'

41 'He will bring those wretches to a wretched end', they replied, 'and he will rent the vineyard to other tenants, who will give him his share of the crop at harvest time.'

42 Jesus said to them, 'Have you never read in the Scriptures:

"The stone the builders rejected has become the capstone;
the Lord has done this,
and it is marvellous in our eyes"?

43 Therefore I tell you that the kingdom of God will be taken away from you and given to a people who will produce its fruit.

44 He who falls on this stone will be broken to pieces, but he on whom it falls will be crushed.'

45 When the chief priests and the Pharisees heard Jesus' parables, they knew he was talking about them.

46 They looked for a way to arrest him, but they were afraid of the crowd because the people held that he was a prophet.

Matthew 21:33-46

Notes on the text

The parable of the vineyard is probably the most important story Jesus told, for it maps out the path which he will follow. The parable is a frightening one for it carries a dreadful warning about the anger of God. Although it was aimed at the Pharisees and the Sadducees (chief priests), as verse 45 indicates, the parable continues to be a challenge to contemporary Christianity.

The story is about a landowner (verse 33), obviously an absentee landlord, who lived in a large house in the city, while his fields were worked by the peasants who rented the farm. That this system was often unfair on the peasants is not the issue in this story. However, we are given to understand that the landowner has provided well for the workers, so that a picture emerges of a generous and caring person. There is on the farm a winepress, a tower for protection and even a wall.

Verse 34 describes how, as was the custom, slaves were sent to collect the rent which in this case was a portion of the harvest. The slaves are attacked and one is even killed. Another group is sent and they are treated in the same way (verse 36). Finally, in desperation, the landlord sends his only son. He thinks that the vine-growers will respect him because, as son, he carries the authority of his father. Instead, the son is murdered — apparently because the vine-growers hope that by killing the heir, the land will become their own (verse 38). In fact, Jewish law disallowed this; unless the owner of the property actually willed it to the workers, they could not inherit it, so the son is killed for nothing.

The false arrogance of the workers is Jesus' way of pointing a finger at the chief priests and Pharisees. They act as if the country belongs to them, but in fact it is God's possession. Time and again, through the prophets, God had reminded the rulers of this fact, but the prophets were beaten up and killed and the message was ignored.

Well, as the audience expected, Jesus tells how the wrath of the father fell upon 'those wretches' and how other people came to take their place in the beautiful vineyard. In Matthew's time there was no doubt about who these 'other people' were. They were the Christians, like Matthew's community. The vineyard was the kingdom of God, growing upon the earth. The rulers of Israel had forfeited their right to God's kingdom through the murder of God's Son (verse 43). In failing to recognise Jesus as the chosen 'stone' (verse 42) they face the threat of judgement by that same stone (verse 44). Part of the judgement was the destruction of Jerusalem by the Romans in 70 AD and the complete loss of any hopes for Jewish independence. Matthew's audience would know and appreciate this aspect. Nevertheless there is a warning for the community too in verse 43. For if they do not bear the fruit of the kingdom, they too will be judged.

The message gets home to the rulers (verse 46), but they cannot touch Jesus for the crowds hold him to be a prophet. The readers of the Gospel, however, know that Jesus is far more than a prophet, for by now they have heard the witness of the disciples. Jesus, as the parable so clearly shows, is the Son of God who comes with the authority of God.

Discussion

We used the parable to lead in to a discussion on the kind of fruit to which verse 43 might refer. We read Matthew 3:8-10 and 7:15-21, applying it to our own context. Then we closed by reading the reflection, and sharing in a time of prayer and worship.

Reflection

Grey stone walls stood silent guard upon the ancient city streets. Crowds jostled hand to hand, face to face, eye to eye. The sounds of the city were people and animals, beggars calling for alms and merchants selling their wares. Angry sounds and sad wails mixed with laughter and joy, with childrens' songs supplying the shrill crescendo — the counterpart to the deep voices of the soldiers.

So he stepped into his own time, bringing a word for his own people. The Son of God, cloaked in human form, chose to walk those dusty streets. Urged on by the pain of the oppression about him, he had no option but to share the suffering. Indeed sharing suffering is integral to God's very nature. Without such a concern, our God would not be the true God.

The pain of rejection, the hate in strange eyes, and the violence of strange hands was not new to the oppressed, nor to the God of the oppressed. But that did not make it any easier or less painful. Not for Jesus and not for his followers. Bearing fruit is a sacrificial occupation.

11. The Confession of the Son

Matthew 16:13-23

The session started with a recap on Matthew's portrait of Jesus as the Son of God. We divided into three groups and were each given a series of references to look up. These included the following:

1   Matthew 3:17
2   Matthew 4:3-6

Hamilton K. Budaza

3   Matthew 8:29
4   Matthew 11:27
5   Matthew 14:33
6   Matthew 26:63-64
7   Matthew 27:40-43
8   Matthew 27:54
9   Matthew 28:19

As for the previous two portraits, the group leader had prepared a poster. The heading for this one was, of course, *Jesus, Son of God*. On the basis of our group discussion and the verses we had looked up, we added our own comments to the poster.

We then shared in a time of praise and worship, focussing upon Jesus as Prophet, King and, particularly, as Son of God. We used the slogans on the poster as keys for our prayers. We sensed the power of God that day and for the first time we were able to say that we were really united.

We read the passage together, with different people taking the parts and a narrator to fill in the gaps. Then we studied the notes.

13 When Jesus came to the region of Caesarea Philippi, he asked his disciples, 'Who do people say the Son of Man is?'
14 They replied, 'Some say John the Baptist; others say Elijah; and still others, Jeremiah or one of the prophets.'
15 'But what about you?' he asked. 'Who do you say I am?'
16 Simon Peter answered, 'You are the Christ, the Son of the living God.'
17 Jesus replied, 'Blessed are you, Simon son of Jonah, for this was not revealed to you by man, but by my Father in heaven.
18 And I tell you that you are Peter, and on this rock I will build my church, and the gates of Hades will not overcome it.
19 I will give you the keys of the kingdom of heaven; whatever you bind on earth will be bound in heaven, and whatever you loose on earth will be loosed in heaven.'
20 Then he warned his disciples not to tell anyone that he was the Christ.
21 From that time on Jesus began to explain to his disciples that he must go to Jerusalem and suffer many things at the hands of the elders, chief priests and teachers of the law, and that he must be killed and on the third day be raised to life.
22 Peter took him aside and began to rebuke him. 'Never, Lord!' he said. 'This shall never happen to you!'

²³ **Jesus turned and said to Peter, 'Out of my sight, Satan! You are a stumbling block to me; you do not have in mind the things of God, but the things of men.'**

Matthew 16:13-23

Notes on the text

Background

Peter's confession of Jesus occurs in all four Gospels, but with different words and nuances. Common to each report is the basic sense of Jesus as the agent of God. In other words, the titles like Messiah (Mark 8:29), Holy One of God (John 6:69) and to a certain extent Son of God (Matthew 16:16), convey the sense that Jesus is the one sent by God — God's special agent. So while we do not know the precise words which Peter used, indeed we have only the Greek version of these Aramaic words, we do know what he intended.

Text

Matthew has recreated Mark's version of the confession in a very skilful fashion. Peter's confession is more developed and the role of the church receives particular attention. In verse 13 we are told where the incident takes place. Caesarea Phillipi is one of the most scenic spots in all Israel, with a fresh rushing spring, tranquil pools, shady trees and beautiful waterfalls. It is a place to take refuge in, to hide away from prying eyes. We can imagine that even at this stage Jesus chose to avoid the urban areas of Galilee, restricting his ministry to the open countryside. Here Jesus and his little group of followers would be safe from prying eyes and informers.

Jesus asks the disciples what their perceptions of him are. The title Son of Man (Child of Humanity) was Jesus' favourite name for himself. It allowed him to identify himself completely with the people about him.

The disciples' replies reflect the common understanding of Jesus. For the ordinary people Jesus was someone *like* John the Baptist, or *like* Elijah or Jeremiah (the suffering prophet). Verse 15 turns our attention to the disciples as the reader is prepared for some new insight. Peter's confession follows and here, in Matthew, this includes the discovery that Jesus is the Son of the living God. Not just the Messiah King, but the one who calmed the storm, Jesus the divine Son of God.

Jesus confirms the correctness of Peter's confession (verse 17) for it is a revelation from on high. God as parent (Father) reveals his/her child (Son). The family likeness shines out for all to see.

Verses 18 and 19 address Matthew's community and the church at large. The word which is translated as church is *ekklesia*, which means 'congregation' or better still 'community'. Jesus is to establish a new community with a distinctive lifestyle and Peter is to play the key role in the whole process. For Peter is the one who will usher the Gentiles into the new community (see Acts 10). Matthew makes sure we are all paying attention. We, the Gentiles, are reminded that it was not by accident that we came into the church but by the express will of God.

Often overlooked is the implication that Jesus and, indeed, God have rejected the previous *ekklesia*, namely the Jewish high priesthood and the Temple. Jesus' words are the death knell for that establishment. For Matthew's community the destruction of the Temple was the fulfilment of this prophecy and a further confirmation that God had chosen them over the Jewish leaders of their time.

The authority given by Jesus to Peter and the reference to binding and loosing and the keys of the kingdom (verse 19) are all part of the same picture. Binding and loosing refers to the right of Peter, and those leaders who follow him, to make rules. But there is an even greater issue here, namely breaking through the barriers imposed by society. Peter is the one who will lead the church through the first boundary, that of race. James would try to lead the church through the barriers of class (James 2). Paul offers a way through the barriers of slavery and restrictions on women (Galatians 3:28).

Still today the struggle continues with the same or similar barriers forcing us apart. The authority of binding and loosing (*cf* John 20:23) continues to be held in the Christian community. The church is called on to expose evil and to break down barriers in the name of Jesus. Indeed one might say that Jesus appointed the church for this very purpose.

The verses that follow (verses 21-23) give an account of Peter's attempt to make Jesus turn aside from his true calling. In Mark this follows immediately after Peter's confession, but Matthew separates the two incidents by including both a blessing on Peter and a reference to time going by (verse 21). Peter is then denounced as Satan and as a stumbling block (literally something which causes one to go back on a promise or commitment). So Matthew separates Peter the confessor from Peter the creator of problems.

Why did Peter take issue with Jesus (verse 22)? Was Peter trying to force Jesus to become a violent revolutionary, winning God's kingdom by force of arms? Or was Peter afraid? Afraid of Jesus' methods because he saw that eventually Jesus would be killed and the disciples persecuted, not only by the Romans but also by the Jewish leaders. The evidence suggests that Peter believed that Jesus would die. He truly did believe it. But he was afraid of what it would mean for the disciples. In the end Peter is protecting not Jesus, but himself.

Finally, unlike Mark's story, Matthew is not only teaching us something about Jesus, but wishes to show us that Jesus, the Son of God, is closely connected with the church-community. All those who recognise Jesus as Son of God are qualified to be members of the community of the new age. Moreover, just as Jesus is the agent of God, so the individual members, like Peter, will become God's agents in this world. The agency of Jesus has been transferred to the church. The essential nature of the church therefore needs to mirror that of Jesus. In other words Christians are called to be like Jesus. So simple, yet so profound.

We notice the promise given by Jesus that not even Hell itself can prevail against his church (verse 18). What a great note of assurance for tiny Christian communities like those of Matthew's time! In the face of the terrible dragon of Roman persecution, Christians could lay hold of this promise and laugh at danger.

Discussion

We shared a discussion on the role of the church as the breaker of barriers, and then applied it to our own experience. How does your church cope with the barriers imposed in your society? What can we do? Together we identified some practical ways in which our group could work for the breaking down of barriers in our land. For example, we decided we needed to meet regularly to share our common experiences. More importantly, we realized that we needed to work together in our pursuit of justice and peace for our land. We also felt that as Christians we needed to make other Christians aware of the kind of things which separate us. Sadly, the very fact of living with barriers often blinds us to their very existence.

Before we closed in prayer we spent some time thinking about the way in which Jesus the Son of God, as presented by Matthew, demands some kind of reaction. We were reminded of the passages which we had read at the beginning of the session. We observed that most of the verses recorded someone's reaction to Jesus. Sometimes they were sceptical and attempted to discredit Jesus, at other times they offered up real expressions of praise and adoration.

We spoke for a while about the amazing way Jesus continues to provoke reaction through his messengers today, both in the realm of social and political concerns and in the realm of personal religious beliefs. Before we closed, we read the reflection and shared our thoughts on the passage.

Reflection
Standing at the crossroads he waited for some sign as to the way he should follow. The darkness of the unknown shrouded the way and left him without sight. Confession or rejection, that was the choice. Why was it that God had removed all the other options? Confession? No that was too costly, it demanded too much of one's time and energy. Rejection? No, that was too dangerous. Hell was such an unpleasant thought. So he waited at the crossroads, hoping that some random chance of fate might throw him one way or another. Like Peter, he stood between confession and rebuke. He knew the words, but struggled with the meaning. Too proud to kneel, too afraid to ask, he stood between life and death in the shadow of the cross.

12. The Everliving Son

Matthew 28:1-10, 16-20

In the last of this series we spent some time looking back and reflecting on the previous eleven sessions. In a relaxed atmosphere, while we waited for some late arrivals, we shared our feelings and impressions. All three posters were on the wall as a reminder of the way which we had trodden together. There was also a fourth sheet which read, Where to now? We would fill this in later in the session.

As we shared our observations we realised how much we had grown as a group. We were no longer strangers. Some of us were now firm friends. But we were still conscious of the barriers between us. One could not overthrow a lifetime of apartheid society in a few weeks or months. Such unity as we strived for grew out of sharing more than just words and ideas. It grew out of sharing each other's lives, and that, especially for white South Africans, required major sacrifices. Nevertheless, we had begun to see that the message of Jesus demanded just that kind of sacrifical lifestyle. We were determined to try!

We read the passage together and then the notes.

1 After the Sabbath, at dawn on the first day of the week, Mary Magdalene and the other Mary went to look at the tomb.
2 There was a violent earthquake, for an angel of the Lord came down from heaven and, going to the tomb, rolled back the stone and sat on it.
3 His appearance was like lightning, and his clothes were white as snow.
4 The guards were so afraid of him that they shook and became like dead men.
5 The angel said to the women, 'Do not be afraid, for I know that you are looking for Jesus, who was crucified.
6 He is not here; he has risen, just as he said. Come and see the place where he lay.
7 Then go quickly and tell his disciples: "He has risen from the dead and is going ahead of you into Galilee. There you will see him." Now I have told you.'
8 So the women hurried away from the tomb, afraid yet filled with joy, and ran to tell his disciples.
9 Suddenly Jesus met them. 'Greetings', he said. They came to him, clasped his feet and worshipped him.
10 Then Jesus said to them, 'Do not be afraid. Go and tell my brothers to go to Galilee; there they will see me.'

16 Then the eleven disciples went to Galilee, to the mountain where Jesus had told them to go.
17 When they saw him, they worshipped him; but some doubted.
18 Then Jesus came to them and said, 'All authority in heaven and on earth has been given to me.
19 Therefore go and make disciples of all nations, baptizing them

in the name of the Father and of the Son and of the Holy Spirit,
²⁰ and teaching them to obey everything I have commanded you.
And surely I will be with you always, to the very end of the age.'

Matthew 28:1-10, 16-20

Notes on the text

The one event which more than any other changed people's perception of Jesus was the resurrection. Recorded in such simplicity, it nevertheless remains the mainstay of Christian belief. The resurrection exploded all previous understandings of Jesus to make way for a totally new insight. Old titles like Prophet, King and even Son of God were transformed simply by applying them to the resurrected Lord.

The story begins on the third day of Jesus' death. The Jewish day began at dusk and not at midnight as we are accustomed to think. So Friday evening marked the beginning of the second day, and Saturday evening the third. Mary Magdalene (a disciple of Jesus whom he had healed from some form of mental illness — demonic possession *cf* Luke 8:2 — and not the prostitute of popular mythology) comes to Jesus' grave. She is accompanied by another Mary, whose full identity is not given by Matthew (*cf* Luke 24:10). No reason is given for their visit.

Recently, Israeli archaeologists have studied the two main suggestions for the approximate location of Jesus' tomb. While there is a great deal of guesswork involved, since the Bible gives us no real clues, a pattern has begun to appear. There are two traditional sites for Jesus' burial, namely the Holy Sepulchre in the northwestern part of the Old City and the so-called Garden Tomb in northern Jerusalem (just outside the Damascus Gate). The most recent finds suggest that the region around the Garden Tomb was a burial ground during the Israelite period, particularly the sixth and seventh centuries BC. The Holy Sepulchre, as evident from the design of the tombs and the type of chisel used on the rock, is part of the cemetery which was in use during Roman times. It therefore appears likely that the latter has the best claim to being near Jesus' original tomb.

Verse 2 alerts us to the fact that something unforseen has occurred: an earthquake caused by an angel rolling the gravestone away. The guards faint (verse 4) and the angel then addresses the women. We need to remember that the angels of the Bible were completely normal in appearance except for their bright clothes and shiny faces.

They did not have wings, unlike the cherubim and seraphim. Since the angel answers the women, we must presume that they asked a question. Perhaps it was a frightened cry of 'Who are you?' or even a question as to the whereabouts of Jesus' body.

The angel reassures them, and then pronounces the most amazing news, the very last thing the women expected to hear. Jesus has been raised by God from the dead (verse 4). Unlike Luke, Matthew follows Mark in having the disciples return to Galilee in order to see Jesus (verse 7). On the way to deliver the message to the other disciples, the women meet with Jesus (cf John 20:11-18). Jesus repeats the angel's message about going to Galilee. Of great significance is the women's response to Jesus, for they take hold of his feet and worship him (verse 9). Once again the divinity of Matthew's Jesus shines through.

According to verse 16, the disciples (presumably more than just the eleven) proceed up to Galilee, to the region where they first met Jesus (Matthew 4:18). Here, on the mountain chosen by Jesus, they meet the risen Lord. Probably we are to think of the site of the Sermon on the Mount, which is also called 'the mountain'. The disciples, like Mary and her companions, respond to the risen Jesus by worshipping him (verse 17). The Christians of Matthew's community could well understand that reaction for they too worshipped Jesus. But for the early disciples on that hill in Galilee, this must have been an awesome experience, rather like that occasion after the storm. Jews were simply not given to worshipping anyone other than God.

Some doubt (verse 17). Is this an allusion to Thomas (cf John 20:25)? Is this an oblique reference to Matthew's own community? Perhaps there were some of these doubters still about? What did they doubt? One suggestion is that they, like Thomas, doubted that Jesus had risen from the dead. Another suggestion is that they are uncertain about whether or not Jesus is divine. Both possibilities are interrelated, for it is the risen Jesus who demands a response of worship. For Matthew, Jesus is the divine Son of God. That is the reason for the Gospel. He/she might well have written, as did John, 'But these (things) are written that you may believe that Jesus is the Christ, the Son of God, and that by believing you may have life in his name' (John 20:31).

In the face of the enormous wave of the coming persecution, Jesus assures his disciples that he has all authority conferred on him by God (verse 18). There is no greater, on earth or in heaven. Not even Caesar!

In Matthew 22:17-21, Jesus was challenged about paying tax to Caesar. Jesus had already argued (Matthew 17:25-7) that the Jews, as sons, should be exempt from paying taxes to the Temple. Now, he challenges the rulers of his time on Roman taxes. 'Give to Caesar what is Caesar's, and to God what is God's'(22:21). This should not be understood as Jesus' defining the areas of Church and State. On the contrary, there is nothing which lies outside of God's jurisdiction. The Jews did not recognise any distinction between civil and religious life. How then shall we understand these words of Jesus?

What Jesus intends is a critique of those who use Roman oppression as a cloak for their own oppression of the people. The things which belong to God are justice and righteousness. These are the very things which the Jewish rulers denied to the poor of their time. The things which belong to Caesar are the evils of society, taxation, oppression and injustice. These are the things which shall return upon Caesar's own head.

So when Jesus speaks in Matthew 28:18 of his universal authority, he is challenging the might of Rome. The disciples are sent out with an authority which has no rival. Their message will destroy the things of Caesar.

In the power of this authority the disciples are sent out to make disciples of all people (verse 19). Here again the mission to the Gentiles is key. This process of making disciples, as Matthew well knew, involved changing both people's lives and their societies. It is both a spiritual and a socio-political action. We are not talking here about disembodied souls (an idea quite foreign to the Bible) but about living people and human communities, who needed to hear and obey the teaching of Jesus.

Finally, Matthew ends the Gospel on a most powerful note, the last chord in a magnificent orchestral concerto. Like a lighthouse in a stormy sea comes the note of assurance, 'And surely I will be with you always, even to the very end of the age' (verse 20). So the child Immanuel, God with us, and the Resurrected Lord stand together. What a message! What a Saviour!

Discussion
After a short time of worship, we turned to the fourth poster and put our heads together to answer the question, 'Where to now?'. The following were some of the issues which we saw as important. In your context, you might find others.

We believed that it was vital that Christians should be united against social and political evils. Of prime importance here was the need to educate Christians about the evils of their own society. So many Christians in our land do not realise what terrible things are being done to people. Secondly, few Christians have learnt to apply what they read in the Bible to their daily lives. Not just to their spiritual lives but to their whole involvement in family, business and society. This was the aim of this series of Bible Studies, and we now saw how important it was to help others along the same path.

Then there was the need to assure people who were suffering as a result of oppressive laws, about God's concern for them. This, of course, implied active sharing of their pain as a living out of this teaching. Jesus did not say 'send others', but 'go!'. The tragedy of South Africa, Northern Ireland, Latin America, the West Bank of Israel (Palestine), is that God is so often identified with the oppressors instead of the oppressed. So we became aware of the urgent need to go and to tell the 'people of the land', that God is on their side. That they are God's special concern, not in spite of their suffering, but because of their suffering.

At the end of this important discussion, we used the reflection to introduce a time of prayer.

Reflection
Dawn shattered night when he came. Victor from the tomb, destroyer of death. The echoes of the explosion of his resurrection may still be heard. In every arm upraised to protect the poor and weak. In every hand stretched out to cover the naked. In every voice that cries out against structural violence. In every step that is taken to right injustice.

God, the redeemer of the poor, raised Jesus to life. God reached down through the turmoil of pain, suffering and exploitation to restore him to his throne on high. And in that action God foretold the exaltation of all those humiliated and downtrodden, of all those robbed of wealth and dignity, of all those who suffer at the hands of others. The resurrection of Jesus will always be a sign of hope for those 'who sit in darkness' (Matthew 4:15ff and Isaiah 9:1-2). But they cannot hope until they hear. They cannot hear if they are not told, and they will not believe until they see the marks and scars of caring.

A Scholarly Note

Academic studies of the Gospel of Matthew are plentiful. The following are just some of the more important works which have influenced the writer of this book. In the English language, three studies in particular stand out. The first is that of Jack Dean Kingsbury, *Matthew:Structure, Christology, Kingdom* (Philadelphia: Fortress Press, 1975) and the second is that of David Hill, *The New Century Bible Commentary: The Gospel of Matthew* (London: Marshall, Morgan and Scott, 1972). But it is the commentary by Herman C Waetjen, *The Origin and Destiny of Humanness: An Interpretation of the Gospel according to Matthew* (San Rafael: Crystal Press, 1976), which takes the honours for opening avenues for contextual study.

For an understanding of the background to Matthew's Gospel and the connection with Antioch, I refer the reader to the work of Raymond Brown. Chapter 8 of his work *The Churches the Apostles Left Behind* (London: Geoffrey Chapman, 1984) deals with the heritage of Jewish/Gentile Christianity in Matthew as 'Authority that does not stifle Jesus'. Raymond Brown has also produced a book with John P Meier, *Antioch and Rome* (New York: Paulist Press, 1983), which deals in detail with the two great centres of early Christendom.

On the subject of Palestine in the time of Jesus, there is a superb essay by John P Brown, called 'Techniques of Imperial Control: The Background of the Gospel Event', which may be found in the volume edited by Norman K Gottwald, *The Bible and Liberation. Political and Social Hermeneutics* (Maryknoll, New York: Orbis, 1983). In the same collection of essays may be found another important work by Robert H Smith entitled 'Were the Early Christians Middle Class? A Sociological Analysis of the New Testament'. Smith deals with the Matthean community amongst others.

I also draw your attention to Michel Clevenot's *Materialist Approaches to the Bible* (Maryknoll, New York: Orbis, 1985), as an excellent guide to doing contextual theology. Albert Nolan's *Jesus before Christianity. The Gospel of Liberation* (London: Darton, Longman and Todd, 1976) is another superb guide to the social situation of Jesus' time, as is Hugo Echegeray's *The Practice of Jesus* (Maryknoll, New York: Orbis).

Finally, in the series *Aufsteig und Niedergang der romischen Welt* edited by H Temporini and W Haase (Berlin, New York: Walter de Gruyter, 1977) volume 19.1 of the second section (Principat), there are two essays by Paul Hollenbach, 'Social aspects of John the Baptizer's preaching mission in the context of Palestinian Judaism' and 'The conversion of Jesus: From Jesus the Baptizer to Jesus the Healer'. In these two essays Hollenbach paints a vivid picture of Palestine in the time of Jesus, drawing attention to the different ways in which Jesus and John the Baptist respond to the social, economic and political pressures of their time.

While this is by no means a complete survey of all the literature on Matthew, hopefully there are sufficent guidelines here for those who wish to explore the world of Jesus and Matthew in more detail than I have allowed. But more than academic tomes, use the sense of your own experience and your own social/political context to dig deep into the pages of the Bible, so as to release the wealth buried there-in. For indeed there is yet much which we do not know or truly understand,

> 'for we stand before a great mountain of knowledge and in our lifetime we can do no more than trample the foothills.'